THE ULTIMATE HANDCRAFTED CHRISTMAS

THE ULTIMATE HANDCRAFTED CHRISTMAS

150 decorations, gifts, cards, and treats to make for a perfect Christmas

ALAN D. GEAR AND BARRY L. FREESTONE

whitecap

First published in Canada in 2005 by
Whitecap Books Ltd.
North Vancouver
British Columbia
V7J 2C4

First published in Great Britain in 2005 by
Collins & Brown
The Chrysalis Building
Bramley Road
London W10 6SP

An imprint of **Chrysalis** Books Group plc

1 3 5 7 9 8 6 4 2

British Library Cataloguing-in-
Publication Data:
A catalogue record for this book is
available from the British Library.

ISBN 1552856887

Designer: Elizabeth Healey
Project editor: Miranda Sessions
Commissioning editor: Marie Clayton

Reproduction by Classicscan, Singapore
Printed and bound by Imago, Thailand

Contents

Introduction

One of the most fabulous things about Christmas is that it offers a wonderful opportunity for using all your craft skills to the full—as well as a being a great time to try out something a little bit different. During our 25 years of working in the crafts arena we have met hundreds of interesting and enthusiastic crafters, and in this book we have collected together some of our very favorite ideas for the Christmas season. Here you will find the very best projects to decorate the tree, table, and home, delicious cookies and treats to welcome your guests, as well as a range of desirable items as gifts for relatives and friends. As you plan and prepare for the festive season, consult this book for exciting ideas and information to guide you on your way and make this important holiday time really special for everyone.

In the first chapter we cover different ways to make your home look really festive and welcoming. Here we have some traditional projects, such as the Hanging Evergreen Wreath, but also some contemporary projects; the enigmatic miniature metal picture frames will look stylish and modern wherever you hang them. Chapter Two looks at projects to decorate the tree—so

why not try out the sumptuous braided baubles, or the pretty felt birds—while Chapter Three looks at projects to decorate the table. Of course, one of the central parts of Christmas is giving gifts to our relatives and friends to let them know how much we have appreciated them over the year. Chapter Four shows you how to make really personal gift tags and cards, and Chapter Five has a selection of gift ideas, including mouthwatering seasonal treats and a classically beautiful Fern-patterned vase.

Most of the projects featured in the book use seasonal materials and simple techniques, so no matter if you are a novice at craft or a seasoned professional, you will find something inside to try. Everything is clearly explained, with a list of the materials you will need, detailed instructions and step-by-step photographs, as well as lavish photography of the finished item.

Packed with festive and creative ideas, *The Ultimate Handcrafted Christmas* is the definitive guide to creating the perfect Christmas. Let us show you how to make yours really special this year.

Alan D. Gear and Barry L. Freestone

Decorating *the* Home

Gourd Fairy Lights

YOU WILL NEED

Dried gourds
(1 for each fairy light)

Metallic paints

Paintbrushes

Scrap piece of card

Bradawl

Plastic card

Scissors

A string of outdoor fairy lights

Epoxy resin

Outdoor fairy lights really do create an enchanting atmosphere for Hallowe'en parties or to decorate a tree close to the house. Bell cups are small dried gourds that are sold for use in dried flower arrangements, usually fixed to sticks which are easily removed. They can be found in either a pale natural wood color or sometimes dyed in bright or deep colors. As well as being useful for floral displays, they make colorful covers for fairy lights. Painting the insides of the cups in bright metallic colors will add an iridescent shimmer when the lights are switched on.

1 Make sure that the insides of the gourds are clean and dust-free. Paint the insides of each gourd with metallic paint, alternating the colors, and leave to dry.

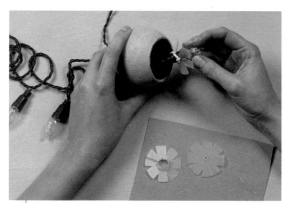

2 Place the gourd on a piece of card to protect the work surface and make a hole in the base of each gourd with a bradawl. Start by piercing the woody base from the right side and enlarge the hole bit by bit. The hole needs to be just big enough for the light bulb to go through.

3 Cut a pair of 1¾in (4.5cm) circles out of plastic card for every light. Make a hole in the center of one card circle just big enough for the wire flex to go through. Make a larger hole in the second circle, big enough to fit around the base of a light. Cut through each circle from the outside edge to the central hole and snip out small 'V' shapes around the outside. Pull a light bulb through the hole in the gourd base and place the circle with the larger hole around the base of the light. Apply glue to the underside of the circle and stick in place inside the gourd, pulling the light and flex back into the cup.

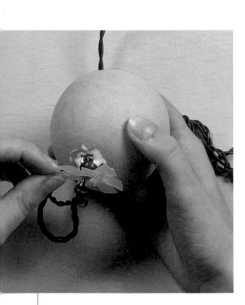

4 Place the second circle with the smaller hole around the flex at the outer base of the gourd and glue in place to secure the light inside. Fix the other lights in place inside the gourds in the same way.

Gilded Candlestick

YOU WILL NEED

★

Large wooden candlestick

★

White wood primer

★

Paintbrush

★

Pale pink water-based paint

★

Very fine sandpaper

★

*Jar of copper colored
gilt cream*

★

2 soft rags

This elegant, tall wooden candlestick has been decorated using a different gilding technique to the one shown on page 44. Instead of using gold leaf, the metal (in this instance, copper) has been mixed into a wax base to produce a fine powder. This makes it a particularly suitable method for gilding complicated surfaces such as the turned candlestick shown here or molded picture frames. It is an ideal project for transforming a tired and familiar household object.

1 If the candlestick is not already primed, apply the white primer and allow to dry thoroughly. Next, apply two coats of pale pink paint and allow to dry. At this stage, you can sand the surface with very fine sandpaper to obtain a smooth finish, if you wish.

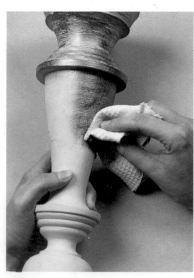

2 Apply the gilt cream to a rag and gently rub into the surface with a circular motion. Don't apply too much at a time as you need to obtain a broken finish where you can see the base color through the gilt cream. Apply solid copper on the flat circular sections of the turned design. When the gilding has been completed, leave the candlestick for 15 minutes, then rub the surface very firmly all over with the clean rag until it shines.

Copper Candle Sconce

YOU WILL NEED

Roll of soft copper foil 4/1000in (0.1mm) thick, 6½in (16.5cm) wide

Tracing paper template (see page 250)

Invisible tape

Dry ballpoint pen

Small, pointed scissors

Piece of card

Sewing tracing wheel

Bradawl

Hole punch

Aluminum can

Strong scissors

Protective gloves

3 brass paper fasteners

Many people would never dream that they possess the skills necessary to work with different metals. However, they are really very simple to learn—no special techniques are required, and some everyday tools have been adapted. This decoration looks stunning placed on a mantelpiece.

1 Cut a piece of copper foil 8 x 6½in (20 x 16.5cm) and lay the tracing paper template on top. Stick in place with invisible tape and draw over the lines with the dry ballpoint pen, pressing very lightly onto the foil beneath to transfer the outline and design. You will need to place the foil on a piece of card or a pile of tissue paper—this provides a yielding surface and protects the worktop.

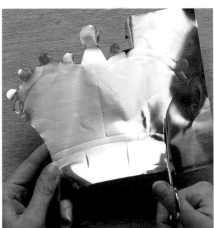

2 Remove the template to reveal the faint impression of the design. Use the small, pointed scissors to cut carefully around the outline, paying particular attention to the small bobbles along the top.

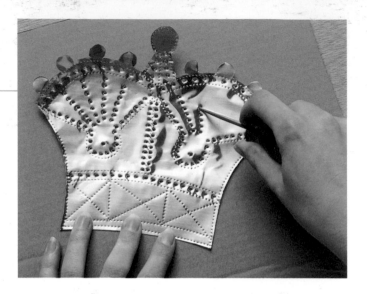

3 Place the crown shape on the card or tissue. Roll the tracing wheel firmly over the transferred lines, add more decoration at this point if you like, then pierce through the copper from the front with the bradawl.

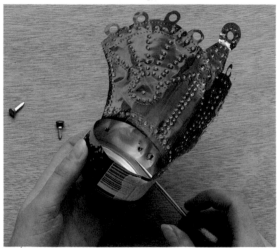

4 Next, using the hole punch, make the larger holes in the bobbles along the top of the crown. You will need to press the handles of the punch together very firmly to produce a neat hole with clean edges.

5 Cut down an aluminum can leaving 1⅜in (3.5cm) upstanding from the base. This is easily done with strong scissors, but you may wish to wear gloves to protect your hands from any sharp edges. Wrap the copper crown around the aluminum can base and, using the bradawl, pierce three holes through both metals.

6 Push each paper fastener through these holes and open out the two arms behind the crown and inside the can, making sure they are pushed firmly back, allowing the crown to stand upright.

Cozy Cove of Treasures
Selling used books, tea cups and other treasures
Facebook & Instagram: Cozy Cove of Treasures

Candle Holder

YOU WILL NEED

★

Template (see page 251)

★

Thin card

★

Scissors

★

PVA glue

★

Nightlight with aluminum holder

★

Papier mâché pulp (proprietary brand)

★

Ready-made decorator's filler

★

Small kitchen knife

★

White recycled paper

★

Fungicide-free wallpaper paste

★

Acrylic gesso or primer

★

2 paintbrushes

★

Pale blue acrylic paint

★

Silver gilt cream

★

2 soft rags

Papier mâché translated from the French means chewed paper. An infinitely adaptable medium, it is inexpensive, lightweight, easy to handle, and requires no special skills or equipment. It has the advantage of being able to imitate other materials such as wood, clay or stone. Papier mâché responds to decorative finishes very well and looks particularly beautiful when gilded.

1 Draw around the template on the card and cut out carefully with the scissors. Place a small amount of PVA glue into the center of the card shape and stick the nightlight holder in place on top. Allow to dry.

2 Mix the paper pulp according to the maker's instructions. Add a little ready-made decorator's filler for additional strength and to prevent shrinkage. Start to build up the pulp over the points of the star up to the level of the nightlight holder. Smooth with the kitchen knife, defining each point into two sides, and allow to dry overnight in a warm place.

3 Tear the paper into small squares, smear lightly with the wallpaper paste and smooth onto the star. Turn under the base. Allow to dry thoroughly.

4 Paint the whole star with two coats of gesso and allow to dry. Gesso is actually a thick priming paint so ordinary acrylic primer will also suffice.

5 Next, paint the primed star with the pale blue paint. Use two coats if necessary to completely cover the holder and set aside to dry.

7 Wait five minutes to allow the gilt cream to dry slightly and then rub vigorously with the rag to distress the surface of the silver and reveal some of the blue undercoat. Finally, polish with a clean rag and place a nightlight in the centre.

6 Working quickly and using a slightly stiffer paintbrush, apply the silver gilt cream all over the surface of the star. Don't worry if some of the blue undercoat is visible.

Honesty Wreath

YOU WILL NEED

Twiggy wreath base

Large bunch of dried honesty

6 silver thistles

Bradawl

*Lengths of florist's wire
14in (35cm) long*

*60in (1.5m) grey satin ribbon
2⅗in (7cm) wide*

Make a welcome change from the rather over-used dark green ivy or holly and predictable red berries by creating this ethereal wintry wreath in palest green and silver to grace your front door.

This unusual and magical combination uses the papery seed heads of honesty and silver thistles which grow so abundantly in the Swiss Alps, opening in dry weather and closing slightly when the air becomes damp like little barometers. The small honesty branches are secured simply by pushing them into the twiggy wreath base, while the thistles are fastened on with short lengths of florist's wire. The garland is then finished off beautifully with a sumptuous gray-green satin ribbon at the top.

1 Break the honesty branches up into smaller sprays and push them individually at an angle into the twiggy wreath base, working around the wreath to make sure the base is well covered. Leave a small space at the top in which to tie the ribbon. You will find that the honesty holds firm and needs no extra form of attachment.

2 Shorten the stems of the silver thistles and make a hole through the top of the stems with the bradawl. Push a length of florist's wire through each stem and twist to hold securely.

3 | Space the thistles evenly around the wreath and secure by pushing the two ends of the wire through the honesty and around the back of the twiggy base. Twist from behind to hold the thistles securely.

4 | Tie the ribbon in a generous bow. Thread a piece of wire through the back of the knot and wire the bow onto the wreath in the same manner as the thistles. The extra wire behind can be twisted into a loop from which to hang the wreath.

Miniature Papier Mâché Houses

YOU WILL NEED

★

Thin card

★

Scissors

★

PVA glue

★

Fungicide-free wallpaper paste

★

Recycled white paper

★

Acrylic gesso

★

Paintbrush

★

Acrylic paint in blue, pink, orange and yellow

★

Selection of silver cord, braids and ric-rac

★

Selection of shaped sequins

★

Adhesive tape

These bright and colorful little houses were inspired by the old Polish custom of making Christmas cribs in the form of houses, churches, and amazing palaces. They were made from card, wrapped in paper, and highly decorated with glittery foils. Groups of carol singers carried the largest examples around the villages at Christmas. The tradition continues to this day and many towns hold competitions to judge the best crib.

1 Draw the elements of the house on to the card—base, back, front, two gable ends, two roof pieces, and roof ridge—and cut out. Using PVA glue, stick the front and sides to the base and to each other. Hold in place for a minute or two until the glue begins to set, then add the front and back sections of the roof, finally adding the roof ridge. Allow the glue to dry.

2 Mix the wallpaper paste and tear the paper up into small squares. Smear lightly with the paste and cover the entire house with paper, taking it under the base. Allow to dry on a radiator or in a warm place for an hour.

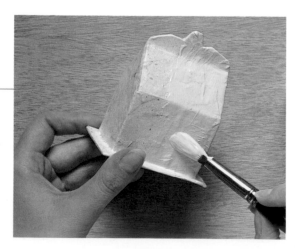

3 Paint the house with two coats of acrylic gesso, allowing it to dry thoroughly between each coat.

4 Mix the blue acrylic paint on a saucer and paint each gable end—you may need to apply two coats for even coverage.

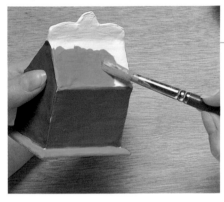

5 Paint the front and back pink, the base and roof orange, and the roof ridge yellow. Always clean the brush thoroughly between each different color.

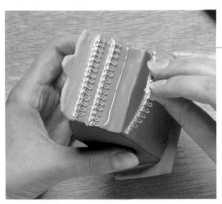

6 Put three strips of the adhesive tape along the front of the roof and stick some of the decorative braid in place. Repeat on the back of the roof.

7 Add the silver ric-rac to the front and back and stick the cord around all edges. Dissect the blue gable ends with a cord length that passes over the roof and down the other side.

8 Lastly, add the sequin decoration, large blue stars at the front and back, and smaller sequins along the roof ridge. Cut the leaves in half and arrange on either side of the silver cord on the gable ends, and finish off with two pink flowers.

Picture Frame Ornaments

YOU WILL NEED

Roll of copper foil 4/1000in
(0.1mm) thick

Small, pointed scissors

Tracing paper template
(see page 251)

Invisible tape

Wad of folded tissue paper

Dry ballpoint pen

Small ruler

Sewing tracing wheel

These enigmatically empty miniature picture frames with their eighteenth-century feel are so simple and satisfying to make, and look quite stunning simply displayed in your home, or even around the branches of your Christmas tree.

Soft copper is easy to cut and enticing medium to work with. It's surprisingly simple to create the lovely repoussé design by drawing on the back of the metal with a dry ballpoint pen, thus making a raised pattern on the front which catches the light beautifully. With age, copper will darken and tarnish; if you want to retain the warm glow of newly worked copper foil, polish regularly with metal polish or permanently protect it from the air with a coat of clear varnish.

1 Cut a piece of copper slightly larger than the template and stick the tracing paper design on with the tape. Rest the copper on the wad of tissue paper and transfer the design onto the metal foil beneath by drawing lightly over the guidelines with the dry ballpoint pen.

2 Remove the tracing paper and press firmly with the ballpoint pen over the lightly drawn lines, using a ruler to help you draw the straight lines. Outline the outer and inner edge of the frame as shown.

3 Draw in the latticework pattern around the frame and fill in the upper part with dots made by pressing the point of the ballpoint pen very firmly into the metal. Remember that you are working on the 'wrong' side of the metal and your design will appear as a raised pattern on the other side. Carefully cut away the scalloped edge in the centre and trim the excess metal around the outside.

Citrus Pomanders

YOU WILL NEED

★

*FOR LINO CUT
ORANGES*

Fresh oranges with firm skins

★

Black felt pen

★

Lino cutting tool

★

*FOR THE CLOVE-SPIKED
POMANDERS*

*Smaller, thin-skinned oranges
(blood oranges are ideal)*

★

Cloves

★

Sharp kitchen knife

★

Lino-cut citrus fruits

Traditional citrus pomanders simply decorated with cloves have been made since the sixteenth century. They were thought to have been carried to ward off disease.

The unusual and inventive variations of Elizabethan pomanders opposite are made by sticking cloves into the orange in spirals, diamonds, and stars. You can then roll them in the ancient recipe of powdered orrisroot and sweet spices to preserve them. This should be done several weeks before Christmas for the best effect. The smaller pomanders are divided into segments with rows of cloves; each segment has been slit with a knife and they have been dried in a cool oven over many days.

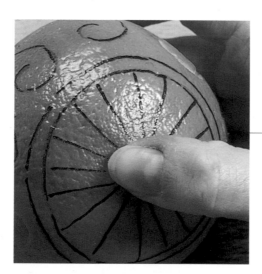

1 Draw the pattern clearly onto the skin of the orange with the black felt pen—simple designs are the best and most effective.

2 Following the lines, carefully cut out the pattern with the lino cutting tool, keeping the blade of the tool moving away from you.

Clove-spiked Pomanders

1 Divide the orange into eight segments with lines of tightly packed cloves. The cloves will push through the peel quite easily.

2 Make long slits in the orange between the lines of cloves. Dry the pomanders in a very cool oven, preferably with the door open, for several days. The coolest oven of an Aga is ideal. A warm airing cupboard is a good alternative.

Christmas Stockings

YOU WILL NEED

*Tracing paper templates
(see page 252)*

Woven red and white fabric

Plain lining

Pins

Scissors

Needle

Thread

Antique crochet

Forget the lumpy and ungracious stockings that everybody expects to see at Christmas and make these really elegant versions to hang in anticipation at the end of a bed or along the mantelpiece on Christmas Eve. Fashioned in the shape of a Victorian boot with antique crocheted, embroidered, or quilted cuffs over lovely red and white woven material, these stockings make long-lasting gifts that may be passed down through generations and used year after year.

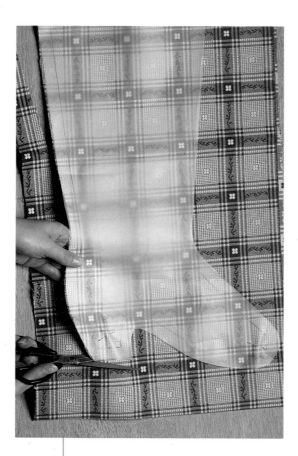

1 Pin the traced pattern onto a double thickness of fabric and cut out. Cut the hanging loop from the red and white fabric and cut two thicknesses of lining.

2 Pin the two stockings together, right sides facing. Using the sewing machine, sew the stockings together, leaving them open at the top. Do the same with the lining. Snip the curved part of the seams so they will turn inside out easily without pulling.

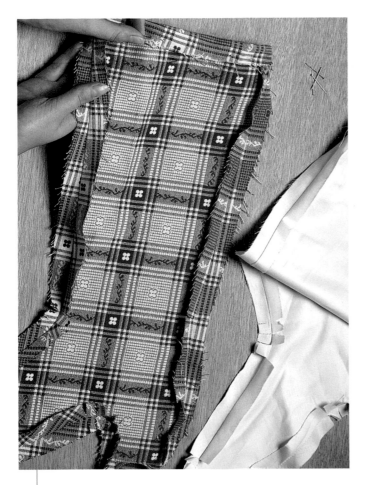

5 | Turn the stocking the right side out and slip the lining inside it, fitting the heels and toes together. Pin together at the top. Neatly stitch the boot, loop and lining together.

3 | Press the seams open on both the lining and the stocking. Turn over a small hem onto the wrong side of the fabric and pin in place. Do the same with the lining and press with a hot iron.

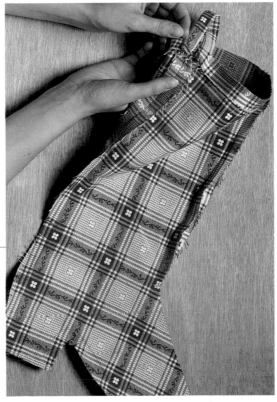

4 | Fold the hanging loop in half lengthways, right sides facing. Sew along the long edge and then turn the tube inside out. Press and pin in place on either side of the back seam of the stocking.

6 | Pin the crochet border around the top of the boot and neatly stitch in place.

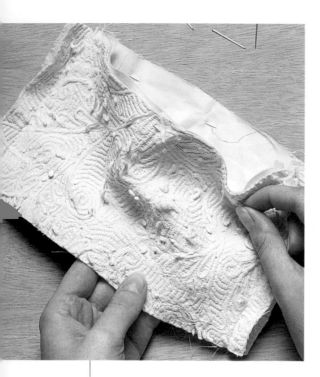

7 To make a boot with a quilted or fabric cuff, use the cuff pattern to cut out two thicknesses of the fabric for the cuff. Cut two linings as well. With the right side of the fabric facing the lining, sew up the two side seams of the lining and cuff fabric. Press the seams open.

8 Turn right side out and slip the cuff inside boot. Pin the top of the boot and stitch in place, enclosing the hanging loop. Pull out the cuff and turn it over the top of the stocking. Press with a hot iron.

Fir Cones

YOU WILL NEED

★

Selection of cones and seed pods

★

Gold spray paint

★

Gold string

There are many ways to add hints of gold to decorative objects. Here is one of the most straightforward techniques to create some classic festive fir cones.

1 Spray a selection of pine cones and other seed pods with gold paint.

2 Tie a piece of gold string onto the end of each bundle for hanging.

Glitzy Paper Chains

YOU WILL NEED

★

Rough paper

★

Gold paper

★

Gold spray paint

★

Ruler

★

Pencil

★

Scissors

★

Sequins

★

All-purpose adhesive

One of the most popular of children's decorations at Christmas, here is a glitzy version to add some glamor to this old favorite.

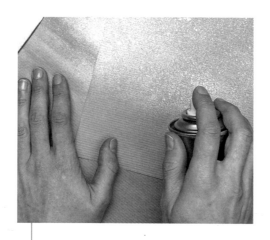

1 Protect your worksurface with rough paper. Spray the back of your gold paper with gold paint so that the insides of the paper chains will glimmer just like the outsides once they are hanging on the tree.

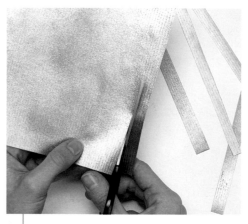

2 Mark faint guidelines approximately ½in (1cm) apart on the paper with a ruler and pencil and then cut the paper into strips.

3 On the outside of each strip, stick a sequin in the middle and at one end for some added sparkle.

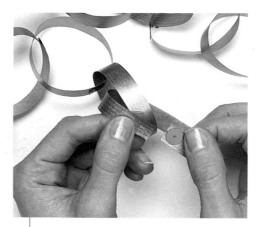

4 Link the strips together, gluing the ends, to make one very long chain or several shorter ones to drape all over the tree.

Cinnamon Bundles

Simple to make, these bundles are especially effective when hung all over the tree, and will create a lovely scent in your home.

YOU WILL NEED

Cinnamon sticks

Craft knife

★

Raffia

Gilt cream

1 Cut the pieces of cinnamon into lengths of about 2in (5cm).

2 Group the cut sticks into fours and tie together using a few pieces of raffia.

3 Tie the raffia ends together close to the bundle to secure, and then again further away from the cinnamon sticks to form a hanging loop.

4 Rub the part of the raffia that is tied around each cinnamon bundle with the gilt cream.

Snowflakes

These glittery snowflakes look wonderful strung together or placed individually on the tree lights or above your mantlepiece.

YOU WILL NEED

★

Silver tissue paper

★

Pencil

★

Scissors

★

Rubber-based adhesive

★

Gold and silver glitters

1 | Cut out small circles of silver tissue paper. These can be all the same size or varying, depending on the effect you desire.

2 | Fold each circle into eight by folding in half, in half again, and then in half one more time.

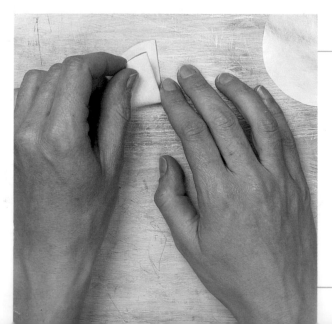

3 | Snip a pattern into each piece of tissue (remember that every snowflake is different). Make the pattern as intricate as you like but don't cut folds away completely or the flake will fall to pieces.

4 | Embellish with glitter stuck on to adhesive. Do this on scrap paper to catch the glitter for recyling. If using the flakes on the lights, switch off and push the flakes well down the outsides of the plastic casings.

Tin Stars

YOU WILL NEED

Template *(see page 251)*

Pencil

Wax

Foil paper

Clear adhesive tape

Ballpoint pen

Scissors

White card

Rubber-based adhesive

Gold glitter

Fishing line

This is the perfect project for young fingers as tracing and using glitter are always very popular crafts with kids.

1 Trace the template on page 251 onto a piece of wax paper. Stick the tracing onto the foil paper using clear adhesive tape and draw over the design with the ballpoint pen. Press hard.

3 Using a tin star as a template, draw around the star onto pieces of white card, allowing a ¼in (5mm) margin around the tin. Spread glue all over the card backings and stick the tin stars in the center.

2 Carefully cut out each star with the scissors (not your best pair as they will be blunted).

4 Sprinkle the card surround with glitter. If you do this over a piece of paper it will be easier to tip excess glitter back into the tube to be used again. Dust off excess glitter and thread with fishing line for a loop.

Tin Angel

Don't be deterred by the length of this project. Although care needs to be taken, the end result is worth it. The little angel can either perch by the hearth or stand at the foot of the tree.

1 | Trace the wings, sleeves, crown, and skirt templates onto wax paper and roughly cut out the shapes. Stick onto foil paper, and draw firmly over the outlines and details with the dry ballpoint pen.

2 | Cut the angel's body from a piece of florist's foam. The finished piece looks like a pyramid with the top sliced off, and the base measures 1½ x 1in (3 x 2cm).

3 | Cut out a small rectangular piece of foil paper and make a hole in the center. Then use the foil to cover the top of the florist's foam body.

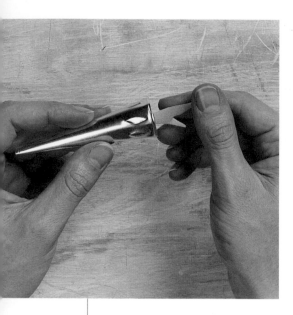

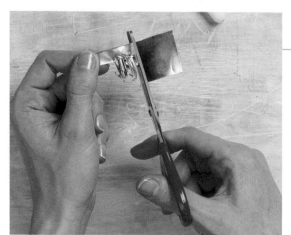

6 | To make the angel's hair, cut out a small rectangular piece of foil and snip along one edge. Stick the hair around the candle with the face on it, ensuring that the fringe is at the front.

4 | Cut out the prepared sleeves from the foil, roll into cones, and fasten on the inside with adhesive tape. Cut the hands from the gold paper and stick with adhesive into the wide end of the sleeves.

7 | Cut out the prepared crown from the foil paper and stick over the hair with the rubber-based adhesive.

5 | Draw the face onto a small oval-shaped piece of gold paper and stick onto the candle. Pare the candle down slightly with a sharp knife if the one you have is too large.

8 | Cut out the prepared skirt, roll into a cone, and fasten on the inside with adhesive tape. Then stick the body and the skirt together using the rubber-based adhesive.

9 For the top part of the angel's dress, wind a string of silver sequins around the body. Start from the waist and work upwards, gluing the sequins into place at the top.

11 Add the head, pushing the bottom of the candle (covered with glue) firmly into the hole made in the foil and through into the florist's foam.

10 Flatten the top of the sleeve cones and fold over ¼in (5mm) to make a hinge. Slot the hinges into the top of the body between the sequins and florist's foam.

12 Cut out the prepared wings from the foil paper and stick them to the back of the angel with the rubber-based adhesive. The top of the wings should be aligned about half way up her head.

Gilded Pot

YOU WILL NEED

★

Flower pot

★

Paintbrush

★

Acrylic size

★

Gold fake transfer leaf

★

Stiff paintbrush

This very clever technique will transform an old pot into a beautiful container. Parts of the pot showing through will give it a more aged look.

1 | Paint the pot with acrylic size. Paint well over the rim of the pot as this area will be very prominent. Leave the size to dry for a few minutes until it is clear.

3 | Gently peel the backing off the transfer leaf. Don't worry if some of the terracotta shows through.

2 | Press on sheets of gold transfer leaf using the stiff paintbrush.

4 | Brush off any excess bits with the same dry paintbrush.

★

Holly Sprigs

YOU WILL NEED

★

Holly

★

Liquid leaf paint

★

Paintbrush

★

Gold glitter pen

★

Fake holly berries

★

Craft wire or florist's wire

Here is an incredibly quick and easy project that combines fresh holly leaves with fake berries.

1 Paint some of the leaves of a sprig of holly with liquid leaf, applying it with the paintbrush.

3 Paint some of the fake holly berries with the liquid leaf.

2 Paint the remaining leaves using blobs of glitter from the glitter pen.

4 To complete each sprig, wire the fake berries onto the painted leaves.

Golden Star

Some very simple folds on gold paper and, hey presto, a golden star to place above your threshold or in a doorway is created.

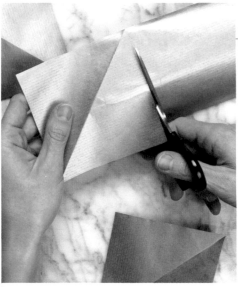

1 Cut out five 4in (10cm) squares of gold paper. Fold each square in half diagonally and open out flat again.

2 On the reverse side, bring one corner to meet the centre fold. Press flat, repeat on the other side and open out. Using the folds, make a 3-D shape, overlapping the outside edges and securing with tape.

3 Repeat with each square of gold paper. Stick the bottom of each point onto a piece of stiff card, butting them up close and placing a piece of adhesive tape under the center points of the stars.

4 Cut out the star, trimming as
close as possible to the gold
paper.

Christmas Potpourri

YOU WILL NEED

★

2 handfuls of assorted cones

★

1 cup of nuts

★

6 cinnamon sticks

★

1 cup of peeled root ginger

★

1 handful of dried orange peel

★

1tbsp (15ml) star anise

★

Cracked nutmegs

★

*Gold-sprayed nigella seed heads
or cones*

Christmas is a time for exciting smells, and this potpourri would be perfect for the hall or living room to greet your guests. Simply place in an attractive bowl once the ingredients are assembled. A recipe has been given below, but you can experiment with your own ingredients.

1 Mix all the ingredients together, except the gold seed heads or cones, and add 2 tbsp (30ml) orrisroot powder. Then add 10 drops allspice oil, 10 drops ginger oil, and 15 drops sweet orange essential oil. Mix all these in thoroughly with a metal spoon.

2 Place the mixture in a polythene bag and seal for two weeks, giving the bag a shake occasionally. Once the mixture is ready, place in a suitably festive container and decorate the top with the gilded nigella seed heads or cones and place in position. If it is placed near a fire or warm radiator, the heat will encourage the perfume to waft around the room.

Apple and Cinnamon Ring

YOU WILL NEED

★

Twiggy wreath

★

3 cooking apples

★

Glue gun

★

All-purpose clear adhesive

★

Cinnamon sticks

★

Essential cinnamon oil

★

Colored ribbon

This ring can be made from simple cooking ingredients you are likely to already have stored for the festive period. A glue gun, though not essential, will make your job a lot easier.

1 Dry apple slices in a conventional oven, on a very low temperature for several hours. For this ring, choose an attractive small twiggy wreath and, using a hot glue gun, attach the apple slices around the ring.

2 Add some whole or broken cinnamon sticks, securing them with the hot glue gun. If you want to increase the cinnamon scent, drop some essential cinnamon oil onto the apple slices.

3 As a final touch, make a decorative ribbon bow in the color you want and attach it to the ring.

Hanging Evergreen Wreath

This festive wreath is ideal if you're short of space on the table—it can be suspended from a hook screwed into the ceiling to give a candelit glow to your dining table while you entertain your guests.

3 | Add several sprigs of holly, again securing them with wire. If the holly is a bit short of berries, you can add some fake ones at this point.

1 | Use wire cutters to snip the hook off a coat hanger. Bend the hanger into a circular shape. Bunch damp sphagnum moss around the wire to a thickness of about 2in (5cm), using florist's wire around it to hold it in place.

2 | Take several bushy branches of evergreen, such as cypress, and arrange them to cover the circlet of moss, overlapping the pieces to cover any stalks. Tie the branches to the ring with florist's twine or wire.

4 | To hang the wreath you will need two lengths of satin ribbon. Each piece should be twice the length of the drop from the ceiling to your hanging height, plus an extra 8in (20cm) for tying around the wreath. Tie each of the four ends opposite one another around the wreath so that the two lengths cross in the center.

5 | Make four bows from the same color ribbon and pin them to the wreath over the four tying-on points.

6 | Gently push a length of florist's wire through each of four red wax candles, approximately ½in (1.5cm) above the bases, as shown.

7 | Position each candle halfway between two bows, and twist the wire around the wreath to hold it in place. To hang the wreath, tie another length of ribbon around the two main ribbons where they cross, make a loop to go over the hook, and tie the ends in a bow.

Ribbon Card Garland

YOU WILL NEED

Red, green and gold gift wrap or ribbon or tinsel

Clothes pegs

Gold paint

This is a fun and simple way to hang up your Christmas cards. Simply take three long pieces of gift wrap or woven ribbon in red, green and gold, and plait them tightly together. Knot them at each end to hold them in place.

1 Now take some clothes pegs, lay them on several sheets of newspaper and spray them with gold paint. Turn them until all the sides have been covered and leave them to dry.

2 Fasten the ribbon to the wall at each end, and use the gold pegs to attach your Christmas cards to it. (If you prefer, and if you have some to spare, you could use tinsel instead of ribbon.)

Shiny Foil Chain

Bright-colored foil paper makes a festive version of the simple link chain. The chains can then be strung above mantelpieces and doorways or used to decorate the tree.

1 Begin by cutting lots of strips about 7 x 1¼in (18 x 3cm). Stick the ends of the first strip together with doubled-sided tape (neater and quicker than glue) to make a link.

2 Now simply thread the next strip through and stick the ends together. Continue in this way, alternating the colors, until the chain is as long as you want it.

Crepe Paper Chain

This simple paper chain takes only a few minutes to make. All you need are
two different-colored rolls of crepe paper and a touch of glue.

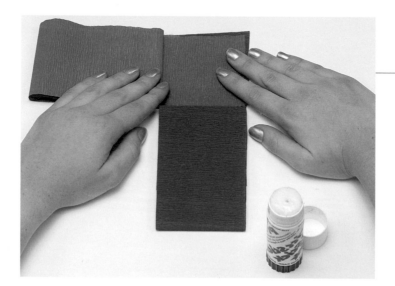

1 | Cut 3in (7.5cm) off the
end of each crepe paper
roll. Place the strips at right
angles to each other, and glue
one end over the other as
shown. Bring the lower strip
up and fold it over the other,
then fold the right-hand strip
over to the left as shown.

2 | That's all there is to it;
just keep folding the
strips over each other
alternately until you reach
the end. Glue them together
at the ends and trim off any
extra bits.

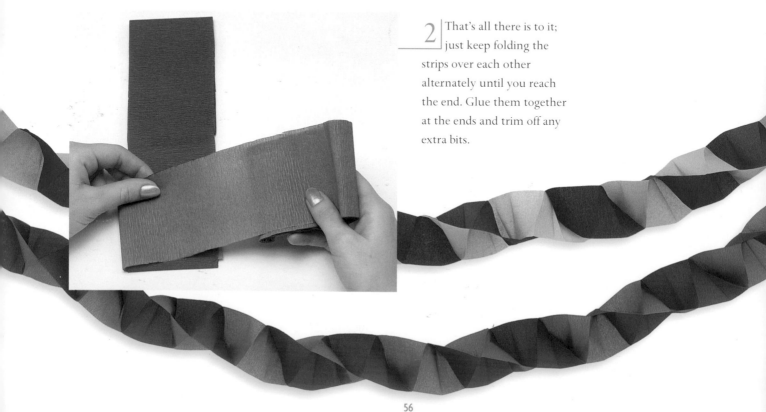

Tinsel Bells

YOU WILL NEED

★

Florist's wire

★

Tinsel

★

Baubles

★

Pliers

All you really need for this decoration is some florist's wire, a little tinsel, and a couple of baubles; but a pair of pliers will make it easier to manipulate the wire.

1 | Bend the wire into the shape of a bell. (You could, of course, try much more complicated shapes once you get the hang of it.) Now wind tinsel around the wire until it is completely covered. A couple of layers will be sufficient.

2 | Finish off with a bauble, tied on to represent the clapper, and some bright red ribbon to tie the bells together.

Holly Wreath

Hang this everlasting wreath on the door for a warm welcome to your visitors. As long as you store your wreath safely you can use it the following year!

1 Cut 2in (5cm) squares of green crepe paper and stick a small piece of masking tape in the centre for extra strength. Cut the point off a cocktail stick and use to make holes in a polystyrene ring. Push each square into a hole with the blunt end of the stick.

2 Continue pushing in squares until the ring is hidden. Take some artificial red berries on wires and push them into the wreath at random to decorate. To finish, add a bow made from ribbon.

Evergreen Wreath

YOU WILL NEED

Evergreen branches

Florist's wire

Small boxes

Christmas paper

Ribbons, bows, gift tags

Add sparkle to a fresh evergreen wreath with exquisitely wrapped, tiny parcels tucked in among the lush green foliage.

1 | Cut branches of spruce or an evergreen tree of your choice and tuck the main branches into a vine base. Following the shape of the wreath, tie in any stray ends using florist's wire.

2 | Collect lots of small boxes. Wrap each box in Christmas paper and decorate with ribbons, bows, and gift tags. Choose an appropriate color scheme—we have used silver and white to give our wreath a frozen, snowy look for winter.

3 | Attach the parcels to the branches or the base with fine florist's wire. Insert it under the ribbons at the back of the parcels, then around the base and twist the ends together.

Dried Fruit and Spices Wreath

Preserve the fall's harvest for a fragrant reminder of its bountiful fruits. It is very easy to make your own dried fruit and vegetables simply by slicing them and drying the slices on a baking sheet in a warm oven for a few hours. They can also be air dried, taking several days to dry completely. Here you can see a selection of suitable ingredients for slicing—including red and green apples plus oranges.

1 Dry baby sweetcorn and chilli peppers in the same way as the fruit slices, allowing a longer time. Make an orange slice 'flower' by wiring the stalks of three or four chilli peppers together, leaving long ends of wire. Insert these down through the center of an orange slice, using the ends of the wire to attach them. Draw round a 10in (25cm) wire frame. Place the fruit and vegetables in position around the ring. Keep this as a plan.

2 Begin on one side and work around the ring, sticking moss onto it with a glue gun. Following your arrangement, start wiring the fruits and trims over the moss using florist's wire. Begin with the larger whole items such as sweetcorn, peppers, and bundles of spices, and attach the wire around the body of the item, bearing in mind the angle that you want to create.

3 | Attach the sliced fruits to the ring in an overlapping arrangement by inserting the wire through the center of the slices. Note that any smaller trims can be attached with a glue gun.

4 | Tie a looped length of raffia string for hanging through the wire at the top of the wreath.

Holly and Ivy Garland

YOU WILL NEED

4 garland cylinders

Sharp knife

Florist's foam

Holly and ivy branches

Newspaper

Adhesive tape

Ribbon

Florist's wire

Greenery, picked fresh from the garden, can be made into a Christmas decoration in moments. To make this lush green design you will need four garland cylinders bought from a florist's shop.

1 Using a sharp knife, cut a block of florist's foam to fit each cylinder, then clip and hook the cylinders together to link them up.

2 Cut branches of holly and ivy to the lengths you require. Trim them, leaving at least a 1½in (4cm) stalk with a sharply cut end to spear into the florist's foam.

3 Fill out the shape of the garland with the holly and ivy, leaving several trails of ivy dangling as if it were growing naturally. Try to give the whole garland the informal arrangement of its natural environment.

4 To make the miniature crackers, cut 2in (5cm) width strips from folded newspaper. Roll each one into a compact 'sausage', fastened with clear adhesive tape, to form the central core. Cut a selection of wrapping papers into 5in (12cm) pieces.

5 Pinch together the ends of paper around the central roll to form the cracker shape and secure by looping a narrow ribbon round twice. Tie the ribbons in a bow, and cut off the surplus paper at the ends of the crackers to neaten them.

6 Thread florist's wire behind the ribbon bows and then twist tightly to form a spear. Push this straight into the florist's foam base to secure the crackers among the leaves of the garland.

Tinsel Card Garland

YOU WILL NEED

★

Template (see page 254)

★

Shiny red card

★

Florist's wire

★

Silver paper clips

★

Silver tinsel

★

Double-sided tape

★

Red ribbon

This star-shaped decoration provides another interesting way to hang your Christmas cards. Make three firm circles, 12in (31cm) in diameter, from florist's wire and bind them with masking tape.

1 Cut three stars out of shiny red card. Position a star in the center of one of the circles and mark the spots where the five points meet the circle.

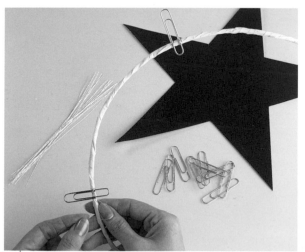

2 Using florist's wire, attach five large silver paper clips to the marked positions, then add another clip in each of the spaces between. Wind lengths of silver tinsel around the rings. Secure the ends of the tinsel in one of the paper clips.

3 Attach double-sided tape to the back of the points of each star and stick them onto the ring to align with the five paper clips. Bind pairs of holly leaves together with florist's wire and stick a narrow bow of red ribbon to them with double-sided tape. Wire the holly onto the ring, between the star points, at the base of a paper clip.

4 | To assemble the garland, place the rings side by side and tie a red ribbon, leaving long ends, around adjoining paper clips on two circles (the joins will be covered by a card). Tie ribbon around the end rings; use the long lengths of ribbon for hanging the garland up. Arrange your cards, using the extended paper clips to hold them in position. Stick a card in the center of each star shape using double-sided tape.

Felt Christmas Tree

YOU WILL NEED

★

Template (see page 256)

★

2 pieces of green felt

★

2 pieces of red felt

★

Batting (wadding)

★

Sewing needle

★

Sewing thread

★

Decorative ribbons and bells

This makes an ideal Christmas wall hanging, particularly if you haven't room for a real tree but still want to add a festive touch.

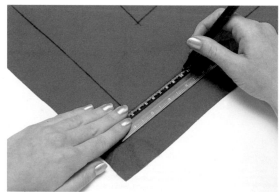

1 First make a paper pattern of a tree, about 30in (75cm) high and 23⅛in (59cm) wide at the widest point across the bottom branches. Also cut a pattern for the pot, about 10in (25cm) high. Make it about as wide as the base of the tree, with a slightly wider, 3in (8cm) deep 'rim' at the top as shown.

2 Cut out two pieces of green felt from the tree pattern and two pieces of red for the pot. Also cut out a piece of batting (wadding) for each. The batting for the pot should be about 1¾in (4.5cm) shorter, since the rim of the pot will be turned down. On the front of the tree mark diagonal lines for the branches as shown.

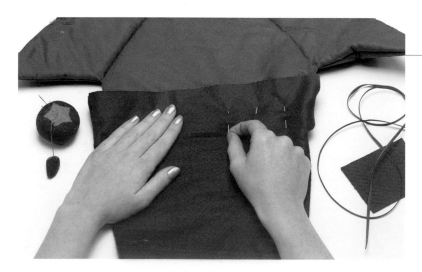

3 Place the tree pieces together, with batting on top. Pin, baste (tack), then stitch ⅜in (1cm) from the edge, leaving the lower edge open. Clip the corners and turn the tree right side out. Stitch along marked lines. Make up the pot, sewing up to 1½in (4cm) from the top. Turn it right side out and slip the tree inside; sew it in place. Sew the upper sides of the pot together and turn the rim down.

4 To decorate the tree, cut out little pockets of red felt and sew them in place as shown. Insert little gifts—either real ones or gift-wrapped card squares.

5 Finish off by adding plenty of ribbons and bells. Curtain rings also look good covered in ribbon and sewn on. Sew a loop to the top of the tree to hang it by.

Star-Burst Candle Lantern

YOU WILL NEED

★

Glass candle lantern

★

Plain paper

★

Scissors

★

Spray glue

★

Turquoise, royal blue, purple, gold, purple, and clear water-based glass paints

★

Paper plate

★

Sponges

★

Craft knife

★

Glass stars

★

Silicone glue

This project is easy to make and stunning to look at. The most time-consuming part is cutting out all the paper masks, so if you have children get them to help. Once this is done, the lantern is quick to make.

1 Photocopy a design as many times as you need and cut out the paper masks. Use spray glue to stick the paper to the glass.

3 Sponge royal blue paint around the base of the lantern. This will blend with the turquoise paint to give a graduated color effect.

2 Sponge on your first color. Start with the lightest colors first, in this case, turquoise. Do not sponge right up to the rim of the lantern. Work quickly so that the paint doesn't dry before you add the next color, or the colors won't blend well.

4 Using a clean piece of sponge, apply purple paint to the rim of the lantern, overlapping the turquoise paint a little.

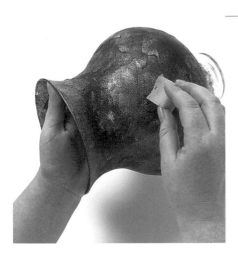

5 | Using another clean sponge, apply a little gold paint around each of the paper masks, and around the base and rim of the lantern.

8 | As a finishing touch, use silicone glue to stick a glass star to the center of each design.

6 | Use the tip of a craft knife and then your fingers to peel off the paper masks.

7 | Finally, using a clean sponge, sponge some clear paint over the clear designs. This will make them look less stark and give a twinkle to the glass when the candlelight shines through them.

Beaded Rainbow Catcher

YOU WILL NEED

Template (see page 255)

Sheet of extra thick film

Gold outliner

Hot stencil cutter

Clear water-based glass paint

Fine paintbrush

Clear, pale pink, bright pink, gold, purple, and blue beads

Silicone glue

Round crystal to fit the hole in the design

Nylon thread

Hang this rainbow catcher in a window and when the sun shines through the crystal in the center, rainbows will appear all over the walls of the room. It is best to make these catchers from rigid, extra thick, plastic film, as glass would be very difficult to cut to shape. Choose translucent and iridescent beads that will catch the sunlight.

1 The extra thick film comes with a protective backing sheet. Peel this off at least one hour before you outline onto it. If you don't do this, the static electricity will make your outliner jump all over the place.

3 Use a hot stencil cutter to cut out the circle in the middle of the design. It is a good idea at this time to check that the crystal fits the hole; it should sit in it without falling right through.

2 Place your design (there are two variation template designs on page 255) under the film and outline it in gold. Leave it to dry and then cut the shape out with sturdy scissors.

4 Starting in the middle, brush clear paint into a few sections of the design. Try not to get paint on the gold outliner or the beads will stick to it and the gold won't show.

5 | Drop clear beads onto the paint. If you fold a strip of paper in half and decant a small amount of beads into this it makes it easier to drop them in the right spot. When you have beaded a few sections, paint a few more and then bead them. Work right around the design in this way.

6 | When all beads are in position, drop some clear paint over them to help hold them in place. Leave to dry for a short while.

7 Add the pale pink beads in the same way. Use the tip of your paintbrush to nudge any stray beads into the right place. Next, add the bright pink beads and leave them to dry. A hair dryer can be used to speed up the drying time, but don't hold it too close, as you don't want to blow the beads away.

9 Place the beaded film over a cup and place the crystal in the hole. Squeeze some silicone glue into an outlining bag and pipe it around the base of the crystal, so that the glue touches the crystal and the film. Leave to dry. When the glue is dry, turn the rainbow catcher over and silicone the back of the crystal in the same way. Leave to dry.

8 Next add the gold beads, followed by the purple beads. Finally, add the blue beads. Leave to dry completely.

10 Then, with a bradawl or hot stencil cutter, make a small hole at the top of the rainbow catcher. Push some nylon thread through the hole to hang the rainbow catcher from.

Granules and Molds

Plastic granules work brilliantly in molds. Choose molds that are simple, strong shapes—you won't get good results from detailed molds as the granules won't go into all the nooks and crannies. You can get lots of molds for free. Next time you unpack your shopping, just see how many products come in plastic shapes. Even yogurt pots and tubs can be used (save the lids to make stencils from).

1 | Grease the mold with margarine, painting it on with a paintbrush. Make sure you cover the whole surface as if any of the granules stick, the shape will be damaged. Remember that a mold only makes half a shape, so for a whole one you need two molds. Here we are making a sphere.

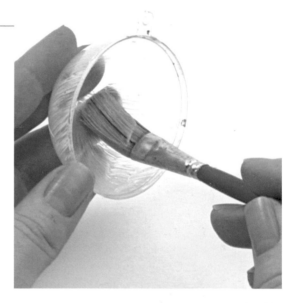

2 | Follow the technique used to mix the granules for the cookie cutters, then spoon them into the mold.

3 | To make a hollow sphere, use the back of a spoon to ease the layer of granules up the sides of the molds. Make the top edges as flat as possible. Leave to dry overnight.

4 | Tap the half-sphere out of the mold. If it sticks, just dip it into warm water for a few seconds and it will drop out. Wash off any grease and dry the half-sphere.

5 | If the edges are a bit rough, place the half-sphere edge-down onto some coarse sandpaper and sand them smoother.

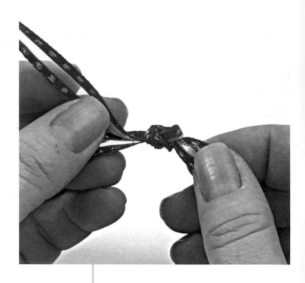

6 | To turn the sphere into a hanging bauble, first knot the ends of a length of ribbon together.

7 | Squeeze some craft or silicone glue around the edge of one half-sphere. Place the ribbon so that the knot is on the inside of the half-sphere.

8 | Press the two half-spheres together to make a whole sphere. Put a strip of masking tape around the sphere to hold it together while the glue dries.

10 | Wind the ribbon around the sphere, covering the join, and glue the other end down. You may find that you need another blob of glue at the bottom of the sphere to hold the ribbon in place. Glue the other length around the sphere at right angles to the first length.

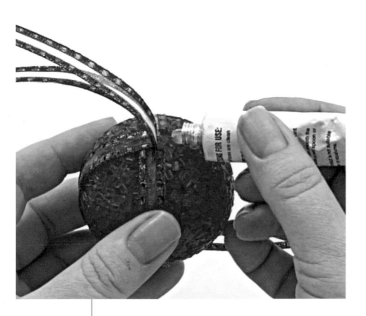

9 | For a neat finish, cut two lengths of ribbon to the same size as the circumference of the sphere. Squeeze a blob of silicone glue onto the sphere on the join, next to the hanging ribbon.

11 | Make tiny gold spots all over the bauble by squeezing on dots of outliner straight from the bottle.

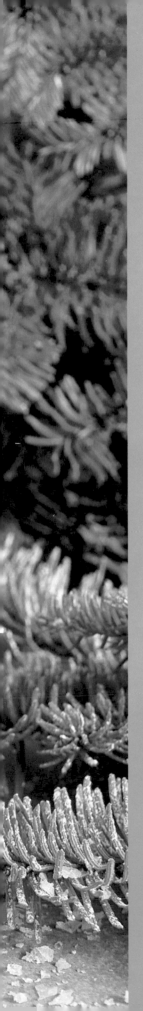

Decorating *the* Tree

Golden Swag

This sumptuous golden swag has the rare and precious feel of an antique fabric. It has been cleverly cut on the bias from exquisite organdie which is loosely woven with silk and metallic threads to produce a stunning, semi-transparent material. Here it has been appliquéd with pale golden ribbons and subtle, gold-sprayed dried flowerheads to enhance your tree at Christmas.

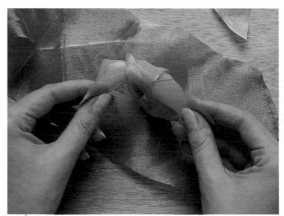

1 Cut a length of organdie on the bias 90in (2.3m) long by 5in (12.5cm) wide. Cut both ends into a point, turn over a small hem and pin to hold in place. Hand stitch neatly with running stitch and remove the pins.

2 Lay a length of gold metallic ribbon across the fabric 4in (10cm) from the end, pin in the middle and stitch firmly in place across the width of the ribbon. Tie the ribbon loosely into a double knot and neaten the ends.

3 Spray the dried flowerheads very lightly with the gold spray to give just a hint of gold. Allow to dry. Lay a flowerhead onto the background 4in (10cm) from the ribbon and stitch in place around the stem.

4 Continue adding ribbons and
flowerheads alternately in this
manner along the whole length of the
swag. Finally, sew the gold tassels in place
on each of the pointed ends.

Glittery Net Hearts

YOU WILL NEED

▲

Template (see page 257)

▲

Scissors

▲

Scraps of colored net

▲

Collection of glittery candy wrappers

▲

Pink, red, and silver sequins

▲

Pins

▲

Needle

▲

Invisible thread

These original and adaptable little tree decorations are so simple and inexpensive to make from scraps of colored net, sequins, and saved candy wrappers. Light and flexible, they can be easily tucked into the branches of your Christmas tree.

The principle of sewing objects in-between two transparent layers could be applied in many different ways—tiny shells between sheets of iridescent cellophane, or miniature jewels enclosed in metallic organdie.

3 Carefully insert six little squares between the two layers of net, pinning through the net (not the paper) to hold each one in place. The sequins are positioned in the same way.

1 Draw a heart on the card and cut out the template. Pin the heart template onto a double thickness of net and neatly cut around.

2 Cut the glittery candy wrappers into small squares, selecting colors of a similar tonal range.

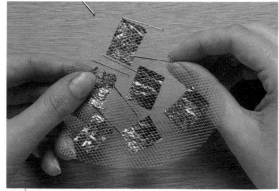

4 Using the invisible thread, sew around each square or sequin, carefully enclosing it between the two net layers. Remove the pins as you sew.

Braided Baubles

YOU WILL NEED

▲

Colored tissue paper

▲

Polystyrene balls

▲

Rubber-based adhesive

▲

Gold cord

▲

Dressmaker's pins

▲

Fancy braid

▲

Sequins

▲

Colored pins

Braids, ribbons, and sequins are held in place quickly and simply with dressmaker's pins, making this project very versatile. You can create quirky or more traditional baubles, depending on your design.

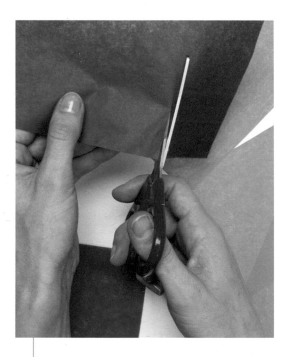

1 Cut out strips of tissue paper that are long and wide enough to wrap around the polystyrene balls.

2 Wrap the tissue paper around the balls and glue into place at the top and bottom with the rubber-based adhesive.

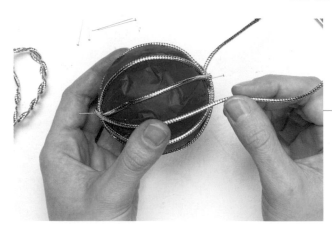

3 Wind the gold cord around each ball to make whatever pattern you want. Use the dressmaker's pins to invisibly secure it, gluing the pins in place to prevent them falling out.

4 Embellish further using fancy braid. Here the braid overlaps alternate strands of the cord, but there are many other ways in which you can use it.

Fabric Star

The brighter the fabric the better. Any colorful material will do, but the two-way colors of silk dupion add style to these tactile and beautifully padded star decorations.

YOU WILL NEED

▲

Template (see page 257)

▲

Stiff card

▲

Scissors

▲

Fabric pencil or chalk

▲

Selection of colored silk dupion

▲

Needle

▲

Thread

▲

Batting (wadding)

▲

Beads, sequins, and braids

▲

Small glass beads

1 Transfer the template onto a piece of stiff card and cut out. Draw around it onto the pieces of fabric (two for each star) using the fabric pencil or chalk. Then cut out the stars.

2 Join together two stars of different colors with right sides facing. Stitch together by hand or with a machine, leaving a small gap for turning through. Turn right sides out and then stuff with batting (wadding).

3 If necessary, poke out the corners with a small pair of scissors as you stuff. Turn in the final opening and sew it up by hand with tiny overstitches.

4 | Embellish the stars with beads, sequins, and braids. For a final twinkle, sew small glass beads onto each point and then hang the stars on the tree.

Felt Birds

The beauty of felt is that there are no fraying edges to contend with. Cut out your shapes and they will remain the same throughout all your Christmases to come.

YOU WILL NEED

▲

Templates (see page 258)

▲

Colored felt

▲

Scissors

▲

Rubber-based adhesive

▲

Paintbrush

▲

Needle

▲

Colored embroidery threads

▲

Batting (wadding)

▲

Blue glass beads

1 Cut out a square of felt, the color that you would like the bird's body to be. Cut out the tail pieces and wings from other colors. Cut a small triangle of yellow felt for the beak.

3 Fold the square over into a triangle and, starting from the end with the beak, sew the two edges together using herringbone stitch in a contrasting colored embroidery thread.

2 Stick the beak onto one corner of the body using the rubber-based adhesive.

4 When you have about 1⅛in (3cm) left to stitch, stuff the bird with the wadding. Do not sew the opening closed.

5 | Roll two different colored tail pieces together. Push the straight end of the tail piece into the body through the hole where the wadding was stuffed and stitch in place to secure.

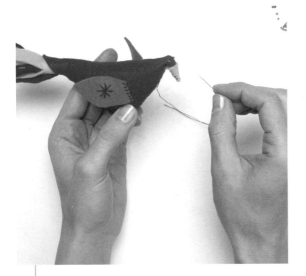

6 | Attach the wings using a contrasting colored thread and then embellish the middle of the wing with an embroidered sunburst shape. Sew on small glass beads as eyes and attach a loop of thread to the bird's back for hanging it from the tree.

Felt Star

YOU WILL NEED

▲

Templates (see page 257)

▲

Green and red felt

▲

Batting (wadding)

▲

Needle

▲

Red and green embroidery threads

▲

Red, gold, and green beads

The embroidery stitches used for this project are straightforward, making the star ideal for a child to make. Colored beads sewn over the edges add a touch of quirkiness to these stars.

1 | Use red for the front, and green for the back and the small star on the front.

2 | Sew the small green star onto the front of the red one using small overstitches and red embroidery thread. Then embellish it with red and gold beads (see the picture opposite for a suggested design).

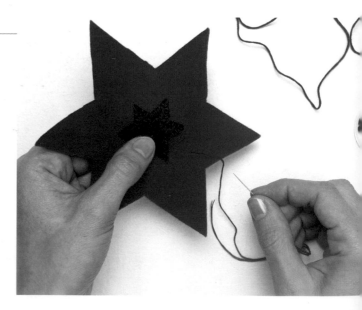

3 Sew a ½in (1cm) wide strip of felt onto the large green star, attaching it at both ends with neat overstitches to form a loop by which to attach the star to the top of the tree.

4 Sew the two sides of the star together using blanket stitch and lightly pad it with batting (wadding) as you go. Thread a bead onto the thread every third stitch or so, alternating the colors in a regular pattern.

Icicles

YOU WILL NEED

▲

Template (see page 258)

▲

Pencil

▲

Wax paper

▲

Scissors

▲

Foil paper

▲

Clear adhesive tape

▲

Ballpoint pen

▲

Glass beads

▲

Fishing line

▲

Rubber-based adhesive

The foil paper that is used for this project and for others in the book is special foil available from artists' suppliers. If you have a garden, these lovely decorations can hang from the branches of a tree.

1 Trace the templates onto a piece of wax paper and roughly cut around the outlines.

2 Stick the tracing onto the foil paper using clear adhesive tape and draw over the detailed patterns using the ballpoint pen. Press hard.

3 Cut out the shapes from the foil paper but don't use your best scissors!

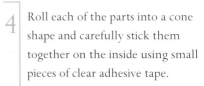

4 Roll each of the parts into a cone shape and carefully stick them together on the inside using small pieces of clear adhesive tape.

5 | Take a piece of fishing line, tie a knot at one end and then thread some glass beads onto it. Thread the other end of the line through the point of the largest cone. Fasten on the inside using adhesive tape.

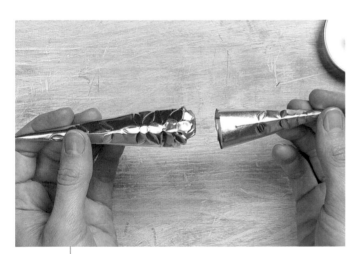

6 | Take a small piece of paper and screw it up into a ball. Then glue both parts of the icicle onto the paper so that the larger piece of foil overlaps the smaller.

Beaded Baubles

Dressmaker's pins are available in different lengths. For this project it is best to use the longest you can find so that you can use a variety of materials to decorate these highly versatile polystyrene balls.

1 Cut out rectangles of foil paper large enough to wrap around the polystyrene balls.

3 Dip the pointed end of the decorated pin into the adhesive. Then push it into the covered polystyrene ball as far as possible so that none of the uncovered pin shows.

2 Thread three cylindrical glass sleeves, a plain glass bead, and a silver sequin onto a dressmaker's pin.

4 Repeat steps 2 and 3 until the whole ball is covered. Add some fishing line in a loop for hanging from the tree. Fasten the fishing line to the ball with a pin stuck in place as before.

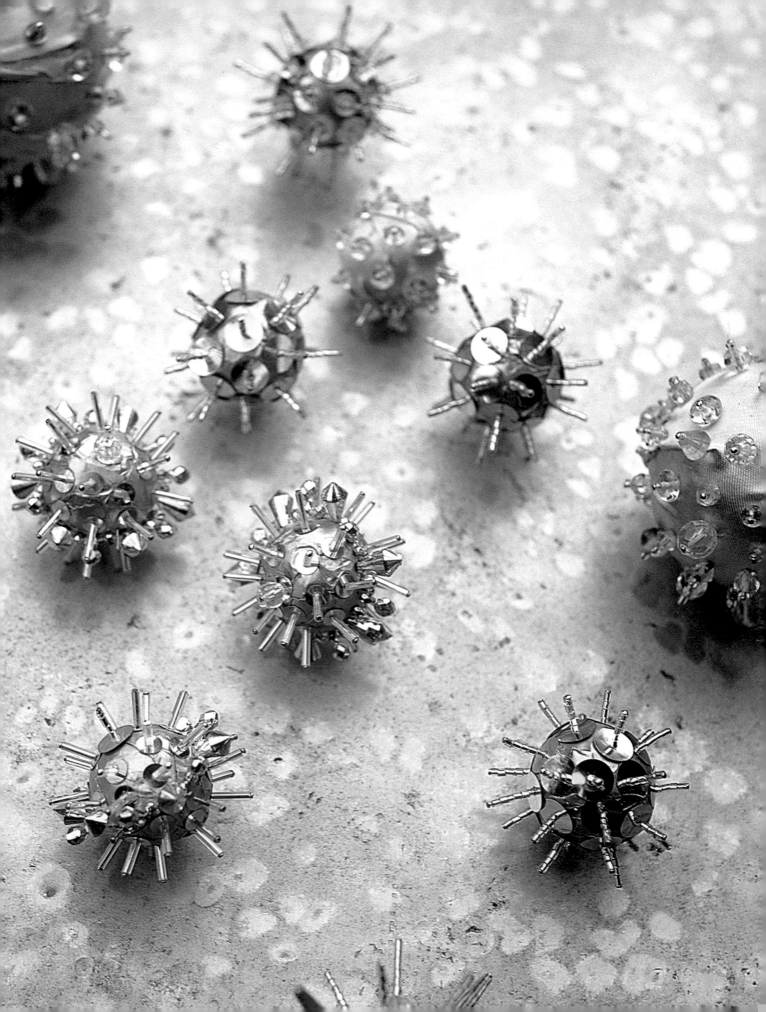

Twinkle Twinkle

YOU WILL NEED

▲

Template (see page 259)

▲

Scissors

▲

Colored thread

▲

Hole punch

This simple star can be hung on the wall or from the ceiling, as well as on the Christmas tree. It is made up of equilateral triangles, which enable the star's points to fold in half to create a three-dimensional shape.

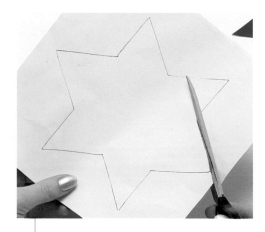

1 | Trace and cut out the template on page 259.

2 | Fold the star in half three times between opposite points. Next fold it in half three times between opposite angles as shown. Every angle and point should now have a fold in it.

3 | The star will now easily bend into its sculptured shape. Make a small hole in its top point with a hole punch or a skewer, then put some thread through the hole to hang it up.

Little Boxes

YOU WILL NEED

▲

Card (see page 260)

▲

Scissors

▲

All-purpose adhesive

▲

Wrapping paper

▲

Ribbons

These little boxes make charming tree decorations. If you haven't got any suitable ones that you can wrap for the tree, you can easily make your own from card, cut from a simple 'Latin cross' template.

1 | For a cube, you need to mark out a Latin cross shape. The lower arm of the cross should be twice as long as the top and side arms. Also add a ½in (1.5cm) border to all arms except the top one for gluing the cube together.

2 | Fold along all the lines as shown, then bring the cube together, gluing all the sides in place.

3 | Now simply wrap the box in attractive paper, and tie it with ribbons and bows to look like a parcel. Pop it on or under the tree.

Satin Presents

These pretty ornaments can be made any size. For a cube shape the pattern is a Latin cross (as shown), the long piece being twice the length of the others; all the other sides must be of equal length.

YOU WILL NEED

Template (see page 260)

▲

Satin

▲

Iron-on interfacing

▲

Thread

▲

Needle

▲

Polyester filling

▲

Ribbons and bows

1 Cut this shape out in satin, then cut a piece of iron-on interfacing, ½in (1cm) smaller all round. Iron on the interfacing. Also iron in creases to form the sides of the cube.

3 Leave one edge open so that you can turn the cube right side out. Stuff it with polyester filling, then slipstitch the opening edges together. Decorate the cube with ribbon and bows, then set it on a branch of your Christmas tree. For a rectangular box, simply widen the long section of the cross. The round box is a purchased box with satin glued onto it.

2 Placing right sides together, sew all the seams, using a small running stitch, cutting into the corners and using the interfacing edge as a seamline.

Santa Faces

YOU WILL NEED

▲

Template (see page 260)

▲

Scissors

▲

All-purpose adhesive

▲

Thread

▲

Sequins

These jolly Santa faces will add Christmas cheer to the tree. They make an ideal project for children as the techniques are simple.

1 | Cut out all the pieces in felt, using the template. Glue the main face piece to a piece of card. When it is dry, cut around it.

2 | All you have to do now is glue on all the other pieces. The nose and cheeks are affixed before the moustache, which goes on top.

3 | Place a loop of thread under the circle on the top of the hat, to hang up the face. Glue on two dark sequins to represent the eyes.

Mini Trees

YOU WILL NEED

▲

Template (see page 260)

▲

Scissors

▲

Colored felt

▲

Thread

▲

Needle

▲

Batting (wadding)

▲

Sequins

▲

Tinsel and gold or silver
thread

Another fun tree decoration that will last from year to year. You can use any of the tree templates at the back of the book , or create your own shapes.

1 | Cut out the tree and pot in card, using the templates on page 260. Now cut the shapes out in two different colors of felt, cutting two each of tree and pot. Place the two tree shapes together, and work buttonhole stitch around the edges, leaving the trunk end open.

2 | Stuff the tree lightly with a little filling. Now buttonhole stitch around the pot, leaving the top open. Slip the trunk into the pot, and then lightly stuff the pot. Sew the tree and pot together at the sides.

3 | Sew a little bow to the top of the pot, and decorate the tree with sequins and tinsel. Fix some gold or silver thread under the star on the top of the tree, so you can hang it up.

Little Parcels

YOU WILL NEED

▲

Thin card or cartridge paper

▲

Adhesive tape

▲

Colored crepe or foil paper

▲

Ribbon

▲

Double-sided adhesive tape

These colorful parcels can be hung on the Christmas tree or on the wall. For a surprise, add a little gift or secret note and insert before you seal the ends.

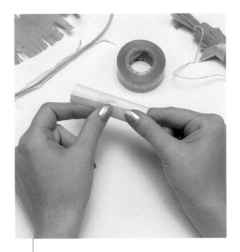

1 First take a piece of cartridge (drawing) paper or light card about 3in (8cm) wide and long enough to roll into a tube. Hold it together with a little adhesive tape.

3 To decorate the cracker, cut some extra, narrow pieces of crepe or foil paper, fringe them at the edges and wrap them around the tube as before. Alternatively, tie a bow round the parcel or stick a silver star in the middle.

2 Cut a piece of crepe paper or foil twice as long as the tube, and roll the tube in it. Stick the edges together with double-sided tape. Squeeze the paper together at both ends, and tie some thread around them. Fluff out the ends and make small cuts in them to make a fringe.

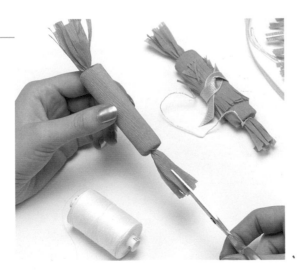

Stocking Fillers

These cute little boots can be used as tree decorations and would also look lovely hanging in front of the hearth.

1 Make a pattern for a Christmas stocking using the template on page 259, and cut it out double in one piece by placing the pattern on the fold of the felt. Cut a strip of fake fur to fit the stocking, about 2in (5cm) deep. Attach the fur to the felt, top and bottom, by hand, with small stitches.

2 Now overcast the two sides of the stocking together, starting at the ankle and working around the foot and up the front. Turn the stocking right side out.

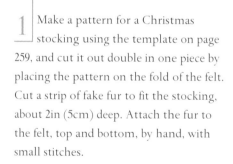

3 Turn the fur down about 1in (2.5cm) to the right side, catching it down around the edge. Decorate the stocking with sequins, bows, etc., and sew a loop of ribbon just inside the edge to hang it.

YOU WILL NEED

▲

Table tennis balls

▲

Fine knitting needle

▲

Paintbrush

▲

Brown paint and varnish

▲

Modeling clay

▲

Thread

▲

Needle

▲

Scissors

▲

Red beads and foil holly leaves

Ping Pong Puddings

Here is another cute tree decoration that is fun to make: tiny Christmas puddings. Table tennis balls are easy to decorate and the perfect shape and size for the tree.

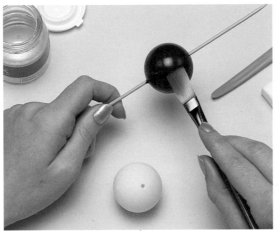

1 You start with ordinary table tennis balls. Spear each one onto a fine knitting needle and paint it brown. After two or three coats, for a dark rich color, finish off with a clear varnish to give the 'puddings' a lovely shine.

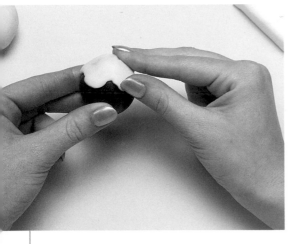

2 Now take some modeling clay, the sort you can bake in the oven, and roll it into a ball, the same size as the table tennis balls. Over this, mold a thick circle of white clay, to look like custard sauce. Bake this in the oven, and then remove it from the clay ball straight away, and pop it onto a pudding.

3 When the clay is cold, glue it to the pudding. Now take a double thread, knot the end and thread it through the pudding from the bottom upwards. Trim off the ends, then finish each pudding by gluing on foil holly leaves and red bead berries.

Let's Pretend

YOU WILL NEED

▲

Lightweight card

▲

Pencil

▲

Colored paint

▲

Thread or ribbon

▲

Tinsel wire

These three-dimensional baubles are simple for children to make and will give a funky retro look to your tree.

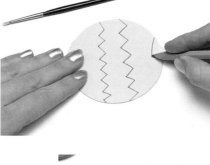

1 First cut some circles, with a little loop on the top, from some lightweight card. Now mark out a pattern on each in pencil. Simple zigzags and curved lines are effective, but not too complicated to fill in.

2 Paint each bauble with several different colors, waiting for each to dry before painting the next. If you have some gold or silver paint, make good use of this, as it is very effective. Use black to make definite lines between colors.

3 When the baubles are dry, attach some thread, ribbon or, as shown, some tinsel wire, so that you can hang them up.

▲

Fairy on the Tree

▲

Foil paper

▲

Scissors

▲

Adhesive tape

▲

Pink pipe cleaner

▲

Doily

▲

Double-sided tape

▲

Table-tennis ball, toothpicks, silver pen

This traditional Christmas tree-top decoration makes a charming addition to the festivities. It can easily perch on the top of your tree without any need for a fixture.

1 Using a saucer, cut a circle out of silver foil paper. Cut the circle in half and fold one half into a cone, stapling it in place.

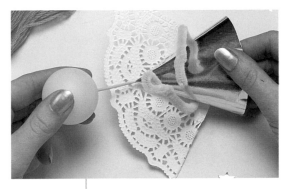

2 Take a pink pipe cleaner and tape it to the back of the cone; then bend it into arms and hands. On top of this fix a triangle of doily to represent wings, using double-sided tape. For the head, take an ordinary table tennis ball and skewer it onto a wooden toothpick (or cocktail stick). Push the stick into the cone.

3 The hair is made from grey crewel or Persian wool, stuck on with double-sided tape, and the crown is a small piece of silver sequin waste. Draw the facial features with a fine-tipped silver pen. For the wand, spray a toothpick with silver paint and stick a small silver star on one end.

Decorating *the* Table

Salt Dough Baskets

YOU WILL NEED

INGREDIENTS

2 cups white flour

1 cup fine household salt

1 cup water

EQUIPMENT

*Small glass bowl to use as mold
(must be ovenproof)*

Oil for greasing the bowl

Rolling pin

Christmas decorations were often made from salt dough in Germany, Switzerland, and Austria in the nineteenth century. The salt was added to the dough as a preservative and to discourage mice from eating the ornaments. A separate tradition exists in South America where examples are brightly painted and varnished.

1 | Mix the flour and salt together in a bowl and add the water gradually. Knead the dough until it resembles firm pastry. Do not add too much water at once as this will make the dough too sticky—if necessary add a little more flour to the dough to make it more manageable. Grease the outside of the bowl very lightly with oil and place it upside down over an object which raises the rim of the bowl off the table. Roll out a small ball of dough, press flat into a disk shape, and place over the base of the bowl.

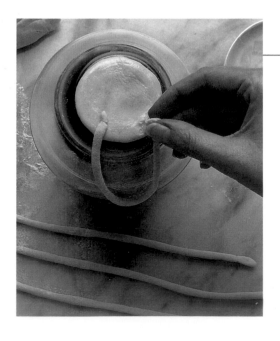

2 | Roll out long sausages of dough to a width of ⅛in (5mm). Wet the outer rim of the base with water—this acts as a 'glue'. Lift a sausage, secure one end to the base and drape the remainder down the side of the bowl in a loop. Attach the other end to the base. Secure both ends into the base by pressing lightly.

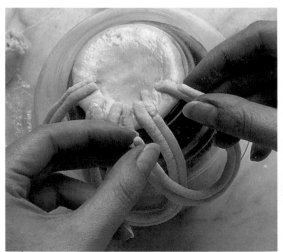

3 | Wet the inside of the loop and make it a double thickness by applying another roll beside it. Each loop starts halfway through the previous loop and ends halfway into the next one—this creates the latticework pattern.

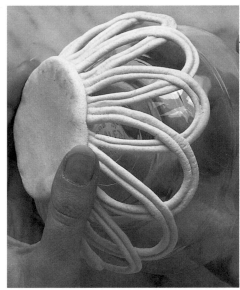

6 Set the oven to a very low heat—250°F/120°C/gas ½. Bake in the oven for about 5 hours or until the salt dough is white and hard. Remove from the oven and allow to cool, then gently release the basket from the mold.

4 After you have completed all the loops, wet the base and cut lightly into the loop ends so they bond with the base and become flatter.

5 Roll out another ball of dough, flatten into a disk, and lay it onto the basket base. Press gently to ensure that it adheres to the dough beneath it.

Copper Placements

For four name plaques

Tracing paper template (see page 250)

Copper foil ⁹⁄₁₀₀₀in (0.1mm) thick, 63in x 8in (160cm x 20cm)

Dry ballpoint pen

Small, sharp embroidery scissors

Wad of tissue paper

Sewing tracing wheel

Invisible tape

Fine, black felt-tip pen

For a really special festive occasion, these beautiful, personalized copper name plaques are surprisingly easy to make. The lightweight soft copper foil is thin enough to cut with a small pair of embroidery scissors. A stunning and really professional effect can be produced with repoussé designs by working on the back of the metal foil with an old, dried up ballpoint pen and a sewing tracing wheel.

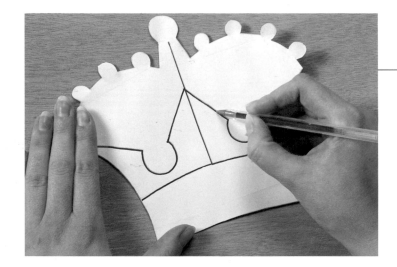

1 Lay the template onto the copper foil and stick firmly in place with tape. Carefully cut around the template with the small embroidery scissors.

2 With the template still in place, draw lightly over the dark lines with the dry ballpoint pen to transfer this part of the pattern onto the copper foil (this is now the back of the plaque).

3 Remove the template and place the copper face down on a wad of tissue paper or similar soft surface. Using the tracing wheel, draw the margin around the crown shape, the lines that were lightly marked through the template, and the tramlines around the space for the name.

4 | Fill in the dots and parallel lines and draw the stars into the bobbles at the top of the crown. Draw around a coin to make circles and draw a central star.

5 | Lay a piece of tracing paper over the area at the base of the crown left blank for the name. With the black felt-tip pen draw in your chosen name to fit the space. Remove the tracing paper, turn it back to front and with the ballpoint pen draw over the letters, using pressure to transfer them onto the back of the metal.

Copper Candle Crowns

Soft copper foil is one of the most rewarding metals to work with, its pliable surface yielding beautifully to the point of a bradawl, resulting in this pierced geometric design. These glowing freestanding copper candle crowns make eyecatching table decorations, ideal for a Christmas Eve dinner.

1 Cut a piece of the copper foil 10in (25.5cm) long by 6½in (16.5cm) wide. Draw on the pattern, as shown, using a chinagraph pencil. Simple geometric patterns are best but vary the design on each crown you make.

3 Using the hole punch, make the large holes as shown in each scallop and along the straight edge of the base. Lay the copper onto the card and evenly pierce holes with the bradawl, using the chinagraph lines as a guide. Take care with rough metal edges.

2 Using the small, pointed scissors, carefully cut around the marked lines of the scalloped edged. A small extra strip on the right edge of the copper has been left to tuck under and make a join when the copper is rolled into a cylinder.

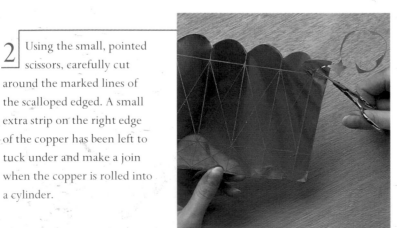

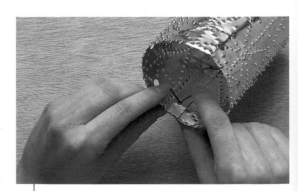

4 When the piercing is complete, roll the copper loosely into a cylinder shape, tucking the extra strip inside at the join. Make three large holes with the bradawl through the two thicknesses of copper and insert the brass paper fasteners.

Beaded Spheres

YOU WILL NEED

Faceted glass or plastic beads, ¼in
(5mm) in diameter

Small iridescent glass beads

Long steel pins

Polystyrene or cotton pulp balls,
1¾in (4.5cm) in diameter

Silk chiffon ribbon

This remarkably uncomplicated project produces spectacular results, resembling the extraordinary jewel-like seeds of the exotic pomegranate. Austrian cut-glass beads combined with a matching beautiful shot-silk chiffon ribbon create a glittering richness which will enhance your Christmas decorations.

1 Thread one tiny glass bead onto a pin, followed by a larger faceted one. As well as being pretty, the tiny glass bead prevents the larger one from slipping off the pin as its central hole may be bigger than the head of the pin.

2 Push the pin into the polystyrene or cotton pulp ball so that the beads lie tightly against the curved surface.

3 Continue pushing the bead-threaded pins into the ball. They should look evenly and tightly packed together in order to conceal as much of the white surface of the ball beneath as possible. Leave a small circular space at the top in which to insert the ribbon.

4 Tie the chiffon ribbon into a small bow, trim the ends neatly with sharp scissors, and insert a pin through the center of the bow. Push the bow into the space that has been left at the top.

Sugarcube Castle

A stunning and unusual idea for a nightlight holder, this fairytale castle is an adaptation of an American East Coast tradition. The whole castle glows white and shafts of warm light filter out from the spaces between the cubes when lit.

1 Make a door frame by sticking together two columns each of four sugarcubes. Stick two more cubes together and insert between the columns and stick in place. Do not use too much glue—a little goes a long way and sets quite rigid after a while.

2 Put the ready-made door frame in the middle of the long side, stick a cube on either side of the doorway and lay the first row of sugar cubes along the black line leaving a small space between each cube, except at the corners. When you come to build the second row of cubes, use the glue to fix them in place with the center of the top cube straddling the two cubes below.

3 Make the window templates from the card by laying four cubes together to make a vertical cross. Draw around and cut out. Insert the templates into the third row on either side of the front door.

4 Continue building up the rows, working around the window templates. Insert the second row of window templates in the seventh row. Make the castellations as shown in the ninth row around the back and sides but continue building the front, creating three gables, one above each window.

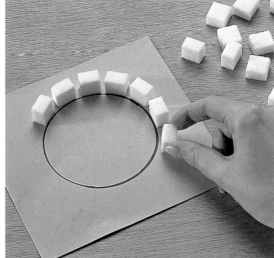

6 To make the tower, use a bowl as a template and draw around it on a piece of paper, making a circle with a diameter of approximately 3½in(9cm). Arrange the foundation row with cubes evenly spaced around this circle.

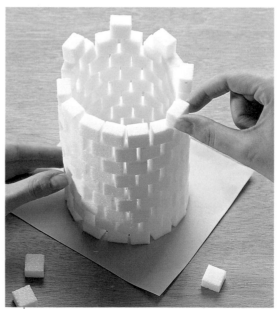

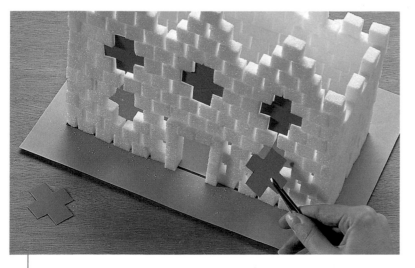

5 Allow the glue to dry for two hours and then remove the templates carefully with tweezers. The window spaces should now be rigid and secure with no fear of collapse.

7 Build up nine rows, then make the castellations on the tenth row by omitting alternate sugarcubes. After leaving to set overnight your castle is now ready to assemble by placing a tower on either side of the main building. To light the castle, put nightlights inside glass holders and place inside the buildings.

Sugared Almond Bags

YOU WILL NEED

✕

Iridescent cellophane

✕

Scissors

✕

Clear adhesive tape

✕

Sugared almonds

✕

Organza ribbon

Small fingers will love filling these bags with sugared almonds, but tying the tops can be fiddly so is best done by an adult.

1 Cut out pieces of iridescent cellophane about 6in (15cm) square.

3 Fill each bag with sugared almonds. Don't put too many almonds into each bag.

2 Stick each piece of cellophane together in the middle and then at one end as if doing up a parcel.

4 Tie each bag at the top with a piece of organza ribbon.

Miniature Pomanders

YOU WILL NEED

Kumquats

Gold thread

Dressmaker's pins

Bradawl

Cloves

Ordinary string

Orrisroot

Sieve

Kumquats make unusual oval pomanders. Their size also complements a small tree. Place in an attractive bowl for a centerpiece.

1 Tie a piece of gold thread around the kumquats to divide them into quarters. Anchor with dressmaker's pins if necessary.

3 Insert the cloves into the holes, pushing them in as far as they will go.

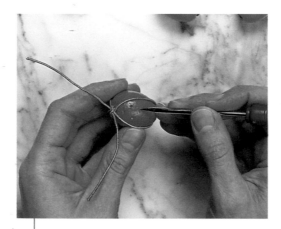

2 Poke holes all over the kumquats with a bradawl or other pointed implement.

4 To use as a moth deterrent, repeat steps 1 to 3, but using ordinary string. Sprinkle with sieved orrisroot and leave in an airing cupboard for 2 weeks. Replace the string with gold thread.

Gilded Physalis

YOU WILL NEED

Physalis

Scissors

Acrylic size

Fake loose-leaf gold

Paintbrush

Gold and orange combine very well, but fake silver leaf is also available and you might like to consider a mixture silver and gold.

1 Spread out the five sepals that surround the physalis fruit and trim to neaten.

3 Press on bits of the loose gold leaf all over the sepals.

2 Paint each sepal with acrylic size and leave for a few minutes until it is clear.

4 With a dry paintbrush, brush off excess bits of the gold leaf and let the adorned fruits dry thoroughly.

Candle Holders

YOU WILL NEED

Nightlights

Florist's foam

Heart-shaped cookie cutter (large enough for a nightlight to fit comfortably into center)

Paper

Wallpaper paste

Acrylic size

Paintbrush

Fake loose-leaf gold

Bradawl

Cloves

Use the template or simply create your own shapes to hold the candle. Placed on the dinner table, the candles will bathe your guests in a magical glow.

1 Cut out a piece of florist's foam using the cutter, or the template on page 257, ensuring the foam is deeper than the nightlight. While still in the cutter, cut a hole from the foam slightly bigger than the night-light.

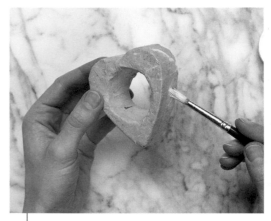

3 Paint the heart with acrylic size and leave for a few minutes until it is clear.

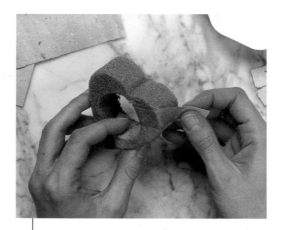

2 Press the foam out of the cutter. Then paste strips of paper over the florist's foam using wallpaper paste. Leave to dry overnight.

4 Press on pieces of the fake loose-leaf gold with your fingers. Do this in a draught-free room.

5 | Carefully and lightly brush off excess gold leaf using a dry paintbrush.

6 | Poke holes for the cloves all around the holder using the bradawl. Then push the cloves into the holes, ensuring they go in as far as possible.

7 | Gently insert the nightlights, and the candleholders are now ready. Do not leave unattended when lit.

Silver Name Places

These attractive decorations form an eye-catching centerpiece, and the surrounding candy makes a delicious accompaniment to coffee at the end of the meal.

YOU WILL NEED

White card

Gold or silver pen

Gold or silver paint

Gold and silver ribbon

All-purpose adhesive glue

1 | For the name tags, cut small squares and rectangles from white card. Trim the edges decoratively, then write the names in gold or silver pen and embellish the edges of the card with silver or gold paint.

2 | Cut lengths of gold and silver ribbon or braid about 6in (15cm) long. Tie a ribbon around one end of each silver tube. Dab a spot of glue on the back of each name tag and press it onto the ribbon.

3 | Pile the gold and silver parcels onto a large plate covered with a gold doily. For a finishing touch, surround them with gold and silver dragées.

Glitter Tree Place Mat

YOU WILL NEED

Template (see page 261)

Shiny green card

Craft knife

Steel ruler

Tiny baubles

All-purpose adhesive

Silver stars

This sparkling place mat is an obvious winner for Christmas. Either use the template on page 261 or create your own design.

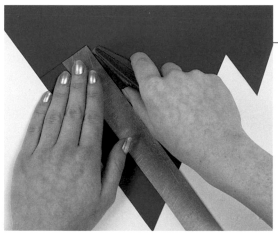

1 First draw a Christmas tree on the reverse (matt) side of a piece of shiny green cardboard. The length should be about 4in (10cm) longer than the diameter of your dinner place and the width 8in (20cm) wider. Cut out the mat using a craft knife and a steel ruler.

2 Add 'ornaments' by sticking tiny baubles to the tips of the tree using strong glue.

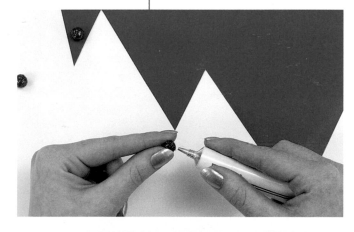

3 Cut out or buy a star shape to put at the top of the tree. Finally, stick small silver stars over the mat. Or, if you prefer, just scatter the stars freely over the mat, first positioning each mat on the table.

Tassel Napkin Ring

This tasseled napkin ring is ideal for a festive occasion. With some colored card and adhesive you can create elegant rings to suit any napkins.

YOU WILL NEED

2 tassels

Colored card

Fabric glue

Scissors

1 Make the ring by feeding the cord through both loops of the tassels twice. Make sure that the ring is large enough to slip easily over the napkin.

2 Using a strong glue, secure the ends of the cord to the back of the ring. Lay one end along the back and trim it. Having applied the glue to the inside of the ring as shown, wrap the remaining end over the cords, covering the trimmed end.

3 Cut the remaining piece of cord on the inside, and clamp it in position until it is dry.

Plaid Place Card

For a traditional Hogmanay or Burns Night celebration, make plaid place cards for your guests. Use plaid ribbon and either white or colored lightweight card, and add a kilt pin for the finishing touch.

1 Cut a rectangle of card about 4 x 5in (10 x 12cm), or a size to fit the place. Fold it in half, and write the name on the left-hand side. Cut a piece of ribbon to edge the card front and back, allowing a little extra to turn under the edges.

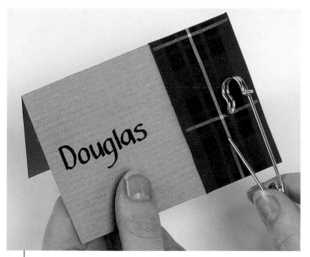

2 Stick ribbon onto the card with fabric glue, folding the excess underneath. Pin the kilt pin through the ribbon and card to complete the authentically Scottish look.

Pastry Place Marker

YOU WILL NEED

Sharp kitchen knife

Water-based paint

Tube paint

Varnish (optional)

Colored ribbon

This pastry place marker has a Christmas theme, but you could easily use a different shape for another occasion. Refer to the basic templates on page 274 to see how to make the pastry.

1 Cut out the tree shapes with a sharp knife or a pastry cutter. Remember to make a hole at the top for the ribbon. Bake the pastry in the normal way.

2 Either leave the shapes plain or color them with water-based paint. You can pipe your guests' names on using tube paint. Varnish the shapes if you wish and attach a ribbon. Note that these pastry shapes are not edible and should be used only for decorative purposes; however, they will keep for years. They can also be used as Christmas tree ornaments.

Frosted Fruit

YOU WILL NEED

N

Pears

N

Grapes

N

Plums

N

Apples

N

Granulated sugar

N

Egg white

N

Ivy leaves for decoration

This stunning centerpiece looks grand enough to grace the most formal dinner party, and yet is very simple to make using an assortment of fruits—here we have used grapes, plums, pears, and apples.

1 Using a pastry brush coat each piece of fruits with egg white.

2 Working over a large plate, sprinkle granulated sugar over the fruit so that it adheres to the coating of egg. Alternatively, the fruit can be dipped into a bowl of sugar, although this tends to make the sugar lumpy.

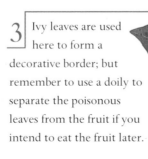

3 Ivy leaves are used here to form a decorative border; but remember to use a doily to separate the poisonous leaves from the fruit if you intend to eat the fruit later.

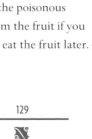

Ivy Candle Ring

YOU WILL NEED

Circular cake base

Strands of ivy

Stems of freesia

White and green candles

Glue or modeling clay

This elegant candle-ring is the ideal centerpiece for a yuletide dinner party. A circular cake base serves as the foundation for the arrangement. Freesia and ivy wrapped around the bowl add a distinctive Christmas appeal.

1 Begin by attaching strands of ivy to the edge of the base, securing them with drawing pins. Build up the ring by adding more strands and bunches of leaves until only a small space remains in the center. Push stems of freesia among the ivy leaves to provide color contrast.

2 Use a mixture of white and green candles of varying heights to form the center of the arrangement. Secure each candle to the base with a blob of glue or modeling clay.

Holiday Centerpiece

For a bright party centerpiece—ideal for Christmas or New Year's Eve—fill a glass bowl with a mixture of shiny glass baubles, foil, feathers, and streamers.

YOU WILL NEED

Glass bowl

Shiny baubles

Streamers

Colored feathers

All-purpose adhesive

Florist's wire

Fine fuse wire

Giftwrap ribbon

1 To make clusters of small baubles, first remove the hanging string. Put a dab of glue inside the neck of each bauble and push in a short length of florist's wire. Leave them to dry.

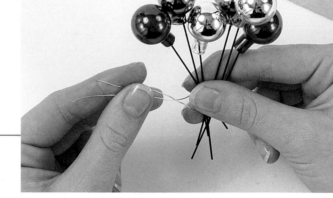

2 Hold the wired baubles in a cluster and wind fine fuse wire around the stems to hold them together.

3 Wrap a piece of shiny giftwrap ribbon around the stems and tie it into a bow. Arrange the baubles and other ornaments in the bowl as shown.

Miniature Christmas Tree

This small fir tree is fun to decorate and makes an unusual table centerpiece. You could also place it almost anywhere in your room—in front of a hearth, inside your front door, in front of windows, or even on a Christmas sideboard.

YOU WILL NEED

 Gold ribbon

 Gold bead strings

 Plaid ribbon

 Fabric glue

 Wide red ribbon

 Small fir tree

 Terracotta pot

1 For a gold tree, make small bows of fine gold ribbon. Drape a string of gold beads in a spiral over the tree, starting at the top, then fix the bows in between the loops of beads.

2 Wrap some tartan ribbon around the pot and secure the ends with fabric glue. Make a separate bow and attach it with glue or pins.

3 For a red tree, cut fine ribbon into 6in (15cm) lengths, tie them into bows and position them on the tree as shown.

4 Tie some tiny red ornaments to the branches; or, if the tree is dense enough, simply place them in the spaces between the bows. Add a wide red ribbon sash around the terracotta pot, tying it in a big bow.

Cone Candle Stand

Believe it or not, this arrangement is quite simple once you get the hang of folding the cones. You need two colors of foil paper in order to create this sophisticated candle stand that catches the light beautifully.

1 Cut out lots of boat shapes 6½in (16.5cm) along the top and 5in (12.5cm) along the bottom and about 2⅓in (6cm) deep. Glue one color to another, back-to-back.

2 Form each boat into a cone and glue it in place. The first few you make may not look too professional, but it doesn't matter; these can go on the outside of the stand and will be partially covered. You will soon get the hang of folding the cones. Bend the bottoms under; it helps to hold the shape and looks tidier.

3 When you have several cones made, start gluing them around the edge of a 8in (20cm) diameter silver cake board. Place another two layers inside the first, leaving room for a chunky candle in the middle.

Forest Foliage

The sideboard, as well as the table, needs a little dressing up at Christmas. This is bright and cheery, and the materials are quite easy to get hold of. If you don't have woodland nearby, your florist should have small sections of bark for sale. Also buy a plastic candle holder.

1 Put a large lump of green modeling clay onto the bark, and stick your candle holder on the top. Now take some plastic or silk fern and spray it gold. Break off pieces when it is dry, and stick them into the Plasticine.

2 When the modeling clay is artistically concealed, pop a red candle in the holder, and set the arrangement on the sideboard. Put a mat under it, though, or it will scratch the surface.

Ribbon Tree

You can really get creative with this small but spectacular ornamental tree—place it where you eat for added color, or even use instead of a real tree if space is limited.

1 First take a medium-sized plastic flower pot, about 6in (15cm) in diameter, and fill it up to about 1in (2.5cm) from the rim with fast-drying cement or wood filler. When this is just setting, insert a piece of ½in (1.5cm) dowelling about 16in (40cm) long.

2 When the filler is dry, spray paint the pot, the dowelling, and the 'earth' surface gold. Lay it down to spray it, and when one side is dry, roll it over and spray the other side. The whole thing—especially the pot—will need a couple of coats.

3 When the paint is dry, take a ball of florist's foam at least 12cm (5in) in diameter and push it on top of the dowelling.

4 Now take short lengths of deep red and green satin ribbon, gold ribbon, shiny baubles, and gold tinsel, and wire them all up, ready to push into the foam. Start with about a dozen of each; you can add to them as you go along, if necessary.

5 Start inserting the wires into the sphere, arranging the ribbons and baubles until it is covered, with no foam showing through. Finally wire up some curling gift wrap ribbon and insert it into the bottom of the ball. (Curl the ribbon by running the blunt edge of a pair of scissors along it.) Wind gold tinsel around the 'trunk' of the tree, and tie a large bow around the pot as a finishing touch.

Decorated Napkins

YOU WILL NEED

Silver or gold spray paint

Blue and white paper napkins

Oil-based crayons

Brush

Here are a couple of ideas for jazzing up ordinary paper napkins to give them a personal touch. The table will look striking with your very own customized napkins. You could use any of the templates in this book, or create your own design.

1 For the blue napkin, cut a star shape from a piece of card—the card must be slightly wider than the folded napkin. Hold the cardboard firmly in place over the napkin and spray silver or gold paint over the area. Let the paint dry for several minutes before you allow anything else to touch it.

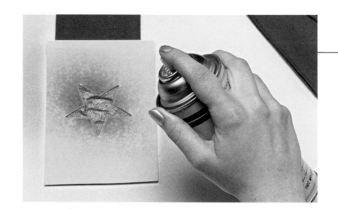

2 The white napkins have a design stenciled on them with oil-based stencil crayons. You can buy these separately or in packs with ready-cut stencils. Choose your design, then place it over the area you want to stencil—in this case the corner of the napkin. Rub the crayon over a spare area of stencil, then take the color up onto the brush and paint it over the stencil in a circular motion.

3 Use the brush only over the parts you wish to show up in that color. Now switch to the next color. It is best to use a different brush for each color if you want clear definition.

Festive Napkin Rings

YOU WILL NEED

Double-sided tape

Colored ribbon

Imitation fur strip

Green felt

Sequins

Satin ribbon

Tinsel wire

These designs for customizing card napkin rings will give a truly individual flair to your place settings.

1 The leaf sprig ring is first covered with a strip of double-sided tape. Cut the tape wide enough to go over to the inside of the ring, and cover the inside with a thinner strip of ribbon. Attach the decoration.

2 Another ring has a strip of fake fur stuck to the outside, to represent snow, and green felt to disguise the card on the inside. Top it with a tiny green felt Christmas tree, sparkling with sequins.

3 Still another idea is to cover the ring with a small strip of wide satin ribbon. Glue a piece of narrower toning ribbon to the inside, folding the edges of the wide ribbon under as you go. Lastly, tie a strand of tinsel wire around the ring and finish with a bow.

Salt Dough Holly Wreath

YOU WILL NEED

Household salt

White flour

Baking sheet

Wax paper

Pastry cutter

Sharp kitchen knife

Red ribbon

Watercolor paint / Varnish

An everlasting plaited heart-shaped wreath that makes a stunning table decoration. You'll want to keep it on display permanently. Refer to page 274 to make the salt dough.

1 Use one portion of dough for the base and one for the decorations. Divide one portion equally into three. Roll each piece into a tube 27in (70cm) long and use them to make a plait. Join the plait into a 11in (28cm) diameter ring, by gently squeezing the ends together.

2 Indent the ring to form the top curves of a heart shape and pinch the lower section to form the point. Place on a baking sheet lined with wax paper and harden in the oven following the instructions on page 107.

3 Roll out the second quantity of dough to a flat sheet ⅛in (2–3mm) thick. Cut out sixteen each of holly and ivy leaves. Use the templates on page 268 if you do not have leaf cutters: trace the outline onto card and cut out. Place the card on the dough and cut round with a sharp knife. Make twelve small balls the size of real holly berries.

4 Arrange the leaves as shown and attach them with dough paste (dough and cold water mixed to a creamy consistency). Dry the decorated heart in the oven.

6 Wrap a long length of red ribbon around the top of the wreath and tie it in a generous bow.

5 Using watercolors, paint the plaited section first, then the leaves and berries, highlighting them with a spot of white paint. When the paint is dry, give the wreath at least two coats of varnish, making sure that the first coat is completely dry before applying the second.

Christmas Ice Bowl

YOU WILL NEED

Glass bowl

Adhesive tape

Seasonal berries

Sequins

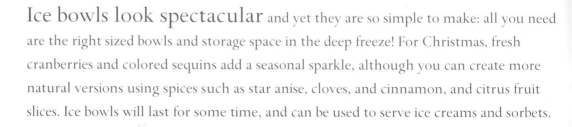

Glitter

Ice bowls look spectacular and yet they are so simple to make: all you need are the right sized bowls and storage space in the deep freeze! For Christmas, fresh cranberries and colored sequins add a seasonal sparkle, although you can create more natural versions using spices such as star anise, cloves, and cinnamon, and citrus fruit slices. Ice bowls will last for some time, and can be used to serve ice creams and sorbets.

1 | Secure a small freezer-proof bowl inside a larger one with tape, leaving a 1in (2.5cm) gap. Fill the gap with berries, sequins, and glitter, then pour in filtered or bottled water.

2 | Leave for several hours until frozen solid. Place bowls in a few inches of hot water to loosen them, then remove the ice bowl and store in the freezer until required.

Woven Table Setting

Christmas colors are woven together to make a matching table mat and napkin ring set that will look charming with all your Christmas decorations and delicious food items on the table.

Cartridge paper

Sticky-backed velour fabric

Craft knife

Green and white paper ribbon

Gold and silver crepe paper

Double-sided tape

Florist's wire

1 From cartridge paper cut out a rectangle 14½ x 10½in (37 x 27cm) and mark a 1in (2.5cm) border all round. Draw lines ½in (12mm) apart across the paper. Cut a piece of sticky-backed velour fabric a little larger all round and peel off the backing paper. Lay the rectangle centrally on top and, using a craft knife, cut through the drawn lines as shown. Fold overlapping fabric over and stick down.

2 Weave lengths of green and white paper ribbon through the cut strips, arranging the ribbon so both ends pass under the border. Fold gold and silver crepe paper into narrow strips and weave over the green and white ribbon. Hold the strips in place with a little double-sided tape at both ends. Trim away the excess paper, then cover the back of the mat with sticky-backed fabric.

3 | Cut a coaster mat from cartridge paper 6½in (17cm) square. Make a border as for the table mat, and mark, cover, and cut in the same way. Weave with two lengths of each color and cover the back with sticky-backed fabric as before.

4 | To make the napkin ring cut a strip from cartridge paper 6½ x 2½in (17 x 6.5cm). Mark out a ½in (12mm) border and divide into strips ½in (12mm) apart. Cover with sticky-backed fabric, and cut strips as before. Weave green ribbon and silver or gold crepe through the slits and secure with double-sided tape. Cut a length of fabric for the backing and stick in place.

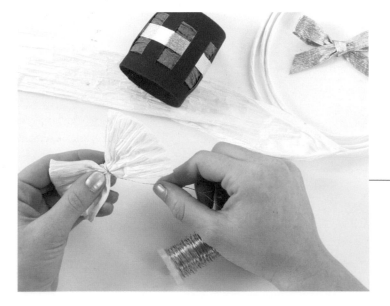

5 | Join the two ends of the ring with double-sided tape. Make a bow shape from white paper ribbon, binding the center with florist's wire. Make a small bow shape from folded gold crepe paper and stick across the white bow with double-sided tape. Stick the completed bow over the join in the napkin ring using double-sided tape.

Santa Napkin Rings

YOU WILL NEED

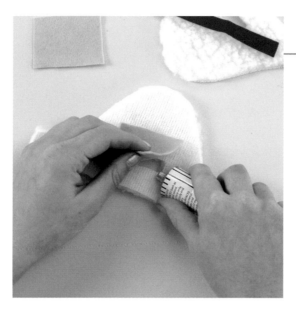

Template (see page 261)

White imitation fur strip

Flesh colored felt

Red felt

Craft eyes

Small bells

Thread

Lay a festive table with a cheery napkin ring for each guest. These fun Santas also make a good crafted project for children.

1 | Cut out one pattern piece (see page 261) from white fur fabric, a piece of flesh-colored felt 2¼ x 1¾in (5.5 x 4.5cm), and a 6 x ½in (15 x 1cm) strip of red felt. Stick the flesh-colored felt centrally across the back of the opening on the fur fabric to form the face.

2 | Now glue the red felt strip across the top of the fur fabric piece. Stick on two small eyes and a square of red felt for the nose. Fold the side panels back to form a ring, overlapping them by ½in (1cm), and glue. Finally fasten a bell to one side of the red band with a length of 'worked' thread, sewing a few strands between the band and bell and working over them with buttonhole stitch.

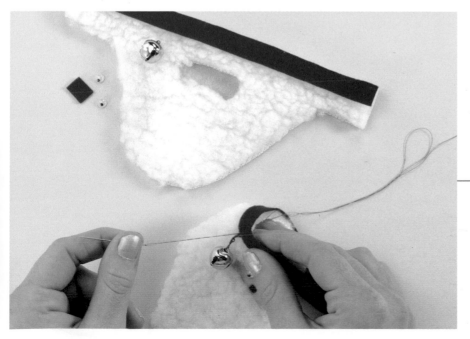

Cards, Tags, _and_ Gift wrap

Embossed Tree Card

Two different embossing techniques are used to make this textural Christmas greeting card. The gleaming foil is in high relief, and the gold powder in low relief. You will need to buy a Christmas tree stamp and special embossing tool.

1 Using the black ink pad, stamp the tree onto the metal foil. Remember to clean the stamp immediately. Leave the ink to dry completely. Working on the stamped side of the foil, draw over all the lines with the thin end of the embossing tool.

2 Turn the foil over and, using the thick end of the tool, work into the inside sections of the tree. This pushes them the other way, so that they stand out on the right side. Start by working along the edges of the lines embossed in Step 1, then work across the sections. You can make embossed lines to suit the shape of design of the stamp you have used. Here, short vertical lines are used to represent the needles on the tree.

3 Working on the stamped side, press the thin end of the tool into the foil around the tree to create a pattern of dots, giving a beaten metal look. You can work the dots in lines or swirls to complement the shape of the stamp.

4 Stick a diamond dot onto each of the raised baubles on the tree.

5 Using double-sided tape, stick the foil to the piece of white mulberry paper. Draw a line around the foil with a wet paintbrush and tear the paper. Pull out fibers to make a fringe. Repeat the process with the green mulberry paper to make a double mount.

6 | Using the gold ink pad and embossing powder, emboss some trees onto vellum. Tear a strip of the embossed vellum approximately 1¼in (3cm) wide. Spray the back with glue and stick it to the left-hand side of the card, close to the fold.

8 | Tear a narrow strip off the front and back edges of the card.

7 | Stick double-sided tape to the back of the foil panel. Peel off the paper backing and stick the panel to the card, just overlapping the edge of the vellum.

9 | Dab clear adhesive onto the torn edges and sprinkle on gold embossing powder. Use a heat gun to melt the powder. The thicker the glue you use, the more textured the embossing will be since the glue bubbles when heated.

Christmas Gift Box

made from the template on page 263.

(see page 263)

YOU WILL NEED

HB pencil

Tracing paper template
(see page 263)

4B pencil

10 x 5in (25 x 12.5cm)
piece of card

Metal ruler

Scalpel

Cutting mat

Double-sided tape

You will really impress your loved ones with these homemade gift boxes, made from the template on page 263. Two presents in one! To alter the size, simply increase or reduce the template on a photocopier.

1 Using an HB pencil, trace the template on page 263 onto tracing paper. The dotted lines on the template indicate where the folds will be.

2 Rub a soft 4B pencil over the traced lines, making sure that you cover both the internal and the external lines.

3 Turn the tracing paper over and place it on top of the card you have chosen for your box. Using a ruler and the HB pencil, draw over the traced lines.

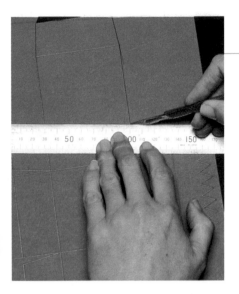

4 Put the card on a cutting mat and, using a scalpel and a metal ruler, carefully cut around the outside edges of the traced lines.

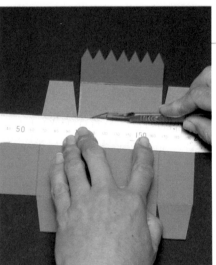

5 Using the reverse side of the scalpel blade, lightly score along the dotted lines. Take care not to press too hard on the scalpel or you will cut right through the card.

6 Press along the fold lines. Place a piece of double-sided tape on each of the four flaps. Peel off the backing tape.

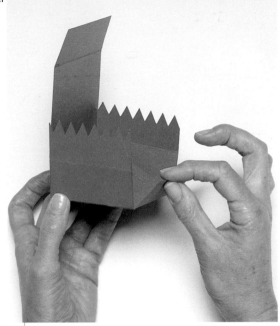

7 Fold up the flaps and press them tightly against the sides of the box to fix them firmly in position. The box is now ready to be filled and decorated. Note: A red-and-green ribbon provides an elegant finishing touch to this simply made gift box.

Snow Scene Card

YOU WILL NEED

8¼ x 12in (21 x 30cm) piece of watercolor paper

Broad paintbrush

Water

Prussian-blue artist's acrylic ink

Ruler

Snowflake rubber stamps

Clear embossing pad

White and silver sparkling embossing powder

Domestic iron

Fabric adhesive

8¾in (22cm) of white pom-pom braid

Decorated with embossed sparkly snowflakes against an inky-blue sky, this is a quick and easy seasonal card that needs few materials. When folded, the card fits a standard-size envelope.

1 Using the broad paintbrush, apply water in a bold, undulating line across the paper, approximately a third of the way up. This will form the skyline, with the unpainted area below suggesting a snowy landscape. Brush water roughly across the upper two-thirds of the paper. For the best results, do not work right to the edges and do not over-wet the paper.

2 Brush on the ink, allowing the color to flood the wet area of the paper. Add more color as required. The ink will gather in some areas, which will dry to a darker shade than others. The effect is random and will be different every time. Leave the paper to dry completely and, if necessary, place it under a few heavy books for a while to flatten it. Score and fold the paper to make a three-panel, concertina card.

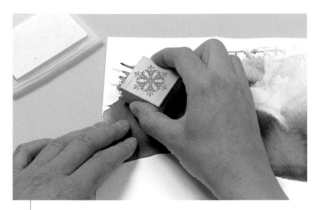

3 Consider the best positions for the embossed snowflakes and stamp the motifs onto the card using the rubber stamps and the embossing pad. Allow some of the motifs to cross onto the white area; the sparkling powder will ensure they show up.

4 Sprinkle on the embossing powder and tip off the excess. Hold the card in front of the soleplate of a hot iron and let the powder melt and fuse together to complete the embossing process.

5 Apply fabric adhesive to the flat part of the pom-pom braid. Stick it to the back of the left-hand panel. Leave to dry and then trim the ends level with the top and bottom of the card.

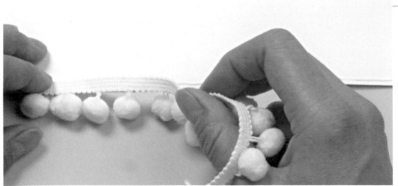

Snowy Christmas Tree Card

If every year you mean to make your own seasonal greetings cards, but never quite manage to find the time, then this is the project for you. You will spend longer writing and sealing them into envelopes than you did making the cards!

YOUR WILL NEED

❦

Cutting mat

❦

Serrated knife

❦

High density stencil sponge

❦

White emulsion paint

❦

Flat dish

❦

8¼ x 4in (21 x 10cm) silver metallic single-fold card

❦

Glue pen

❦

Small colored cup sequins

❦

All-purpose adhesive

❦

Gold star sequin

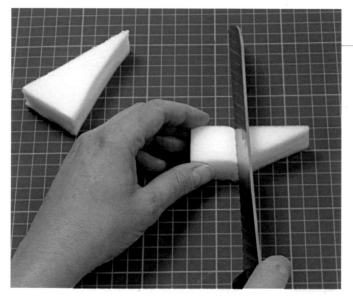

1 Working on a cutting mat, use a serrated knife to cut the sponge into an elongated triangle to make a simple Christmas tree shape 3½in (9cm) tall and 2in (5cm) across at the base. From the off cuts, cut a 1 x 1in (2.5 x 2.5cm) square, which will make the base and the trunk of the tree.

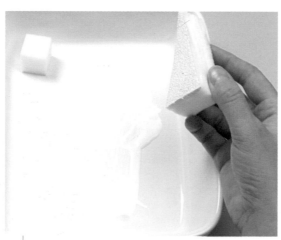

2 Decant some white paint into a flat dish and spread it out thinly. Dip the face of the triangular sponge into the paint, ensuring that the surface is evenly covered.

3 Press the triangle onto the front of the card, positioning it centrally and with the point approximately 1½in (4cm) down from the top. Gently lift the sponge off the card, being careful not to smudge the print.

❦

4 Coat the face of the square sponge by dipping it into the white paint. Make the pot by stamping a square centrally, about ½in (1cm) below the tree. The trunk is made with the same square sponge held at an angle to make a narrow line, joining the tree to the pot. Leave to dry completely.

5 Use a glue pen to stick on a few sequin baubles and a dab of all-purpose adhesive to attach the star to the top of the tree.

YOU WILL NEED

*Tracing paper template
(see page 262)*

Scissors

Steel ruler

Paper glue

Making Envelopes

The envelope you present a card in is important; your efforts will not be set off to best advantage by a tatty envelope! If you can't find a suitable ready-made envelope, have a non-standard size card, or if you want to use a particular paper to co-ordinate with a card, then making your own envelope is the best option. You should also consider decorating the envelope to match the card.

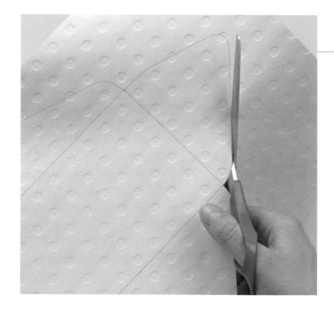

1 Trace a template and transfer it onto the wrong side of the paper. Using scissors, cut out the envelope. If you are nervous about cutting straight lines, use a craft knife and steel ruler on a cutting mat to cut the long straight edges and cut out the curves with scissors.

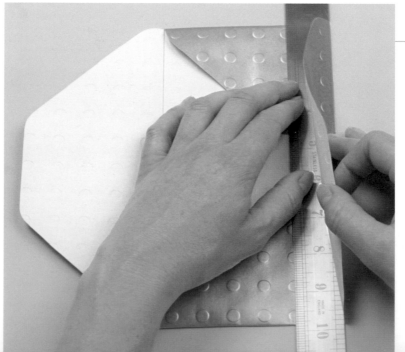

2 With the paper right-side down, lay a steel ruler along one of the crease lines indicated on the template. Lift the flap up and fold it over the edge of the ruler to make a neat crease. Repeat on all four sides to make four flaps, then open the flaps out flat again.

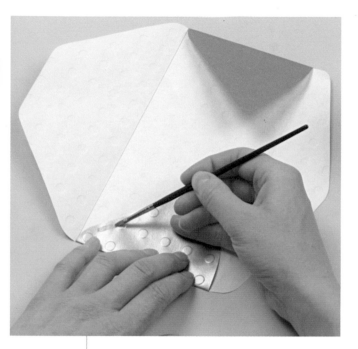

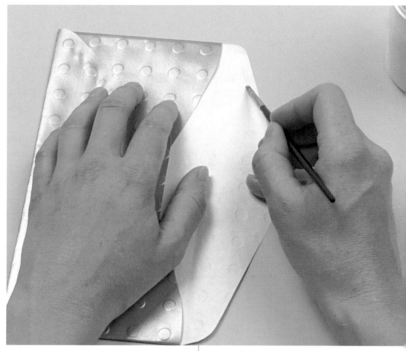

3 | Fold in the two side flaps only and apply a thin line of paper glue or special re-moistenable adhesive—along the edges that will be overlapped by the lower flap. Fold the lower flap up and press it down onto the glue. Leave to dry.

4 | The card can be sealed into the envelope in two ways. You can stick the top flap down with paper glue once the card is in the envelope, or you can use re-moistenable adhesive, as shown here. Paint a thin line of the adhesive along the inside edge of the top flap and leave it to dry. When you are ready to seal the card in the envelope, moisten the flap in the usual way to reactivate the adhesive, then stick the flap down.

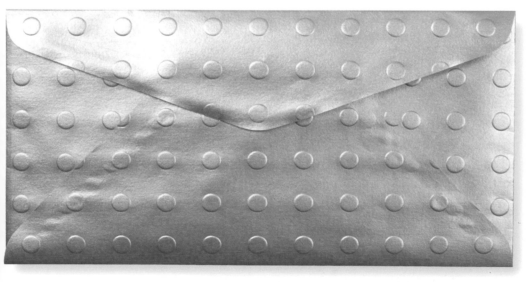

Pillow Envelopes

YOU WILL NEED

Tracing paper template
(see page 264)

Card

Tracing wheel

Ruler

Scissors

Bone folder

Double-sided tape

A card with three-dimensional elements will be spoiled if it is squashed in a flat envelope. Such cards are best hand-delivered in a pillow envelope, which is easy to make from thin card. Enlarge or reduce the one you choose on a photocopier as required.

1 Trace the template and lay it on the right side of the card you want to make the envelope from. Run a dressmaker's tracing wheel over the template outline and crease lines to transfer them onto the card underneath. The indented lines will help you score the card and you do not have to make pencil marks that might be difficult to rub out. Use the wheel against a ruler along the straight edges and be careful not to make marks where they aren't needed, as you won't be able to remove them. Be especially careful around the indents, as the wheel can be tricky to maneuver around tight curves.

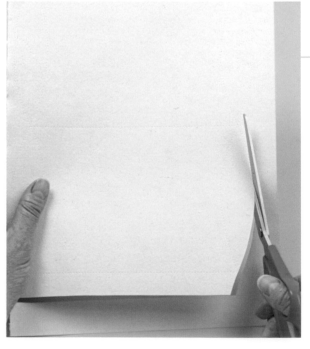

2 Remove the template and cut around the outer edges of the envelope with scissors, following the indented lines.

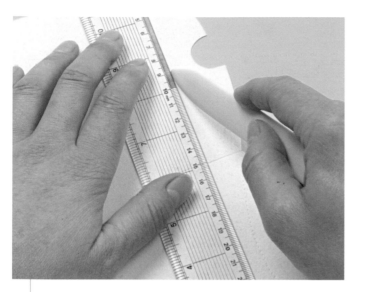

3 Using a bone folder and ruler, score the curved and straight lines indicated by the remaining indented lines. The scoring will cover the indentations made by the tracing wheel, so it is important to be accurate. Along the curved lines, move the ruler around a bit at a time, so that it is always against the indentations and guiding the bone folder. To keep a scored line as smooth as possible, don't lift the bone folder off a line until you reach the end of it.

5 Fold the extended flap in. Fold the taped edge over it and press it down to ensure that the tape sticks to the card right along its length.

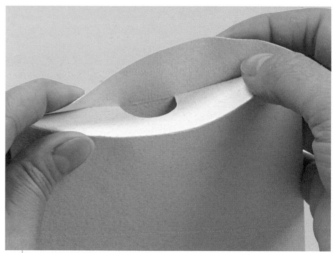

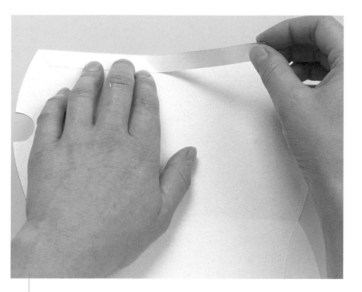

4 Lay the envelope face down. Stick a strip of double-sided tape along the edge without the extended flap, trimming the tape at both ends where it meets the score lines so that it does not overlap them. The tape must not be wider than the extended flap or it will not be covered when the envelope is assembled. Peel the protective paper off the tape.

6 Use your fingers and thumbs to gently press on either side of the curved scored lines to help coax the end sections over. The sections with the indents must be folded over first, so that the envelope can be opened easily.

YOU WILL NEED

Template (see page 264)

4 x 6in (10 x 15cm) piece of tracing paper

4 x 6in (10 x 15cm) smooth pink card blank

Star hobby punch

Dressmaker's pin

Sharp embroidery needle

Lime green stranded embroidery thread

Purple flat sequins

White opalescent star sequin

Colorful Christmas Card

A modern interpretation of a favorite festive motif, this card can be worked in colors to suit your own Christmas theme. You could also try using the same techniques with other simple seasonal shapes, such as stars or snowflakes.

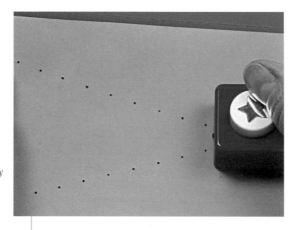

1 Trace the template onto the piece of tracing paper. Lay the paper over the card and punch out the star.

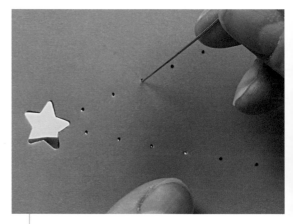

2 Using a pin, pierce holes through the card at the points marked on the template.

3 Thread the needle with a long length of embroidery thread and tie a knot in one end. Push the needle through the top left-hand hole, from back to front, and pull the thread through right up to the knot.

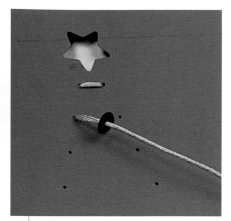

4 | Take the needle down through the top right-hand hole to make the first stitch. Bring it back up through the next left-hand hole, thread on a sequin, then push the needle down through the parallel right-hand hole.

5 | Continue, threading sequins onto each stitch, until the tree is complete. Fasten off the thread on the back. With the card closed, glue the star sequin through the star aperture to the inside back of the card.

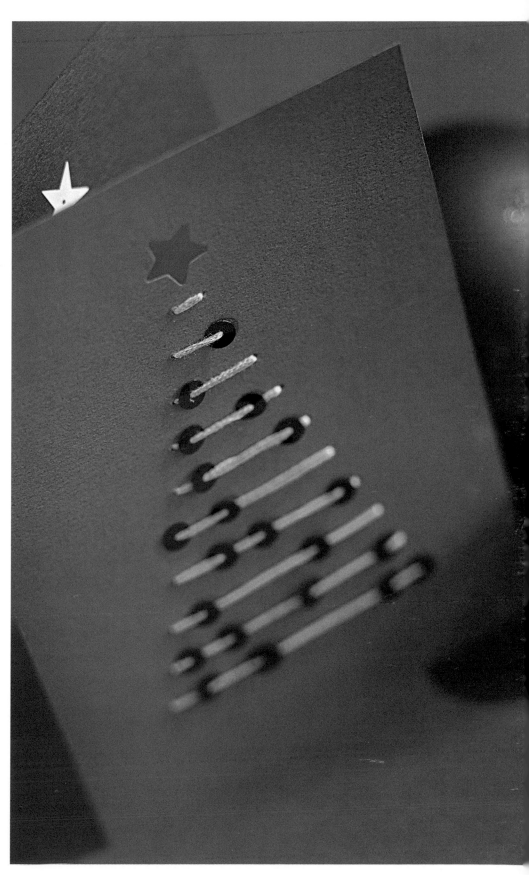

*12 x 4in (30 x 10cm) piece of
black smooth card*

Steel ruler

Bone folder

Cutting mat

Sewing machine

*Multi-colored machine
embroidery thread*

Black tape

Scissors

All-purpose adhesive

4 large star sequins

Glue pen

Cocktail stick

Tiny star sequins

Shooting Stars Card

This dramatic card could be used for sending Christmas greetings or as an invite to a fireworks party. Invent cards for other occasions by changing the motif and colorway; heart-shaped sequins on a pink background for a valentine, perhaps.

1 Score the card 3⅜in (8.5cm) from one short end. Machine curving lines from the score line across the short, front section of the card, using the main picture as a guide.

2 Fold the threads on the leading edge to the back and lay lengths of craft wire over them. Using black tape, tape the wire in place: on the front the wire should continue the lines of stitching.

3 Trim the wires so they are different lengths, both shorter than the back of the card. Put a dot of all-purpose adhesive on the back of a large star sequin and lay the end of a wire on it. Lay another sequin on top. Repeat the process with the end of the other wire.

4 Using the glue pen, put some tiny dots of adhesive on the front and the inside back of the card, positioning them around the lines of stitching and wires. Dampen the end of the cocktail stick, pick up tiny star sequins and put them on the dots of adhesive.

Christmas Gift Card

Like all projects where large quantities are involved, it's best to set up a mini production line; preparing the squares, tying the ribbons, sticking the motifs to the cards, and so on. Best of all, split the tasks between the family and have a jolly evening getting into the festive spirit.

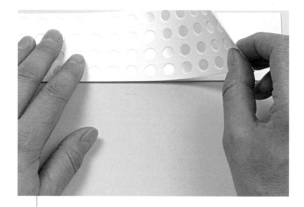

1 Cut a 2⅛in (5cm) strip of wallpaper, taking the placing of the pattern into account. Using paper glue, stick the wallpaper to an identically sized piece of the thick card.

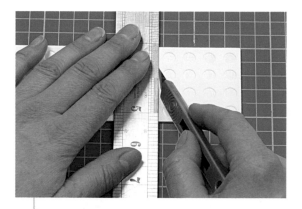

2 Using the craft knife and steel ruler on the cutting mat, cut the strip into 2⅛in (5cm) squares.

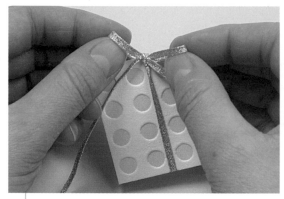

3 Lay a length of ribbon around each square and tie the ends in a bow on one side. Trim the ends.

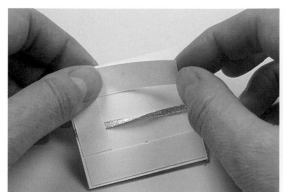

4 Working on the back, stick double-sided tape around the edges of the square. Peel off the backing, and stick to the card blanks, as shown. Use the glue pen to stick sequins in some of the spots.

Christmas Tree Card

If you want to make your own Christmas cards but are put off by the quantity needed, this project is the solution. Do all the stamping first, followed by cutting and folding and finally all the detailing. Make the stamp to fit the cards.

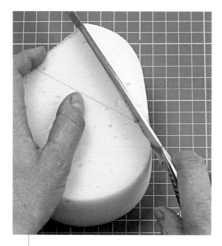

1 Using the felt-tip pen, draw a triangle on the bath sponge. Cut out the shape with the bread knife carefully to keep the edges straight, and never cut toward your hand.

2 Spread some paint onto the plate. Using the paintbrush, brush green paint onto the surface of the sponge. Brush the paint on quite thickly.

3 Stamp the triangle onto the inside front of the card. The triangle must be centered on the card front for the design to work. Leave to dry.

4 Lay the ruler down the middle of the tree. Score lines down the card from the top to the tip of the tree, and from halfway across the base of the tree to the bottom of the card. (The line must be parallel to the leading edge of the card, so ensure that the top line touches the tip of the tree, but if the bottom line isn't exactly halfway across the base, it doesn't matter.)

5 | Using the craft knife on the cutting mat, cut from the scored line at the top of the tree, down the right-hand side, and across the bottom to the scored line at the base of the tree. Cut just beyond the green edge so that the tree has a white border. If you are not confident about cutting freehand, use a steel rule to cut against.

6 | Fold the front of the card back on itself, folding it on the scored lines so that the tree comes to the front.

7 | Punch some small holes within the tree shape. Attach a star sequin to the top of the tree.

Simple, Elegant Card

Wallpaper

Scissors

Paper glue

This is a great way to give cards the elegant, embossed effect associated with complex or time-consuming processes. It looks most convincing when the wallpaper matches the color and texture of the card. As well as making stylish Christmas cards, this is good, inexpensive technique for wedding invitations and formal stationery.

1 Select the section of the wallpaper you would like to use and cut it out roughly. Using sharp scissors, carefully cut out the embossed pattern. The more neatly you do this, the better the card will look.

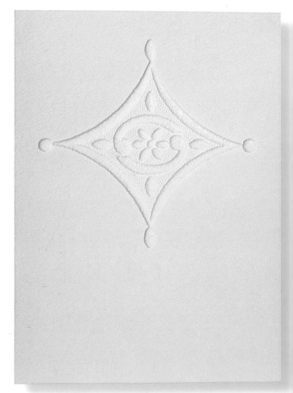

2 Spread paper glue on the back of the cut-out section, making sure that you apply the glue right up to the edges. Stick the section to a matching-color card.

Starry Gift Wrap

YOU WILL NEED

Craft knife

Masking tape

Card for template

Gold spray paint

Silver spray paint

Stenciling is an easy and effective way to decorate paper. Draw a simple motif on card to use as a template and cut it out. Trace around the motif at random on stencil board.

1 Use a craft knife and a cutting board to cut out the stencil shapes. Place the stencil over the paper and hold in place with masking tape.

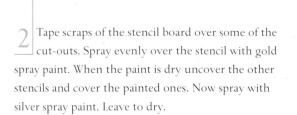

2 Tape scraps of the stencil board over some of the cut-outs. Spray evenly over the stencil with gold spray paint. When the paint is dry uncover the other stencils and cover the painted ones. Now spray with silver spray paint. Leave to dry.

Three Stars Card

YOU WILL NEED

Hobby punch

Double-sided film

All-purpose adhesive

Scrap paper

Colored glitter

With the same attributes as double-sided tape, double-sided film comes in sheet form in a range of sizes, making it especially useful in applications where tape is too narrow. Try cutting it with decorative scissors, using it to stick down larger motifs or to bond fabric to card.

1 Using a hobby punch, punch three circles out of a sheet of double-sided film.

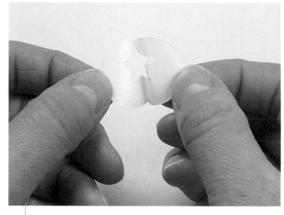

3 Peel the backing off one side of the circles of film.

2 Turn a star hobby punch upside down so that you can see where you are punching. Slide each circle into the punch and punch out a star.

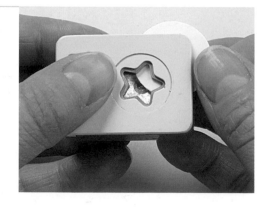

4 Stick the circles onto the card, arranging them as you wish.

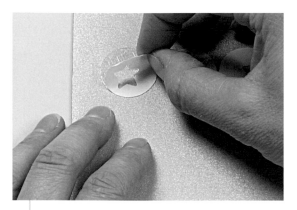

5 Peel the remaining backing off just one of the circles to reveal the sticky film.

8 Tip the excess glitter off onto the scrap paper. Fold the paper into a scoop and pour the glitter back into the pot to be used again. Repeat the process with each circle. Peeling off one covering at a time allows you to make each circle a different color.

6 Lay the card on a sheet of scrap paper to catch the glitter.

7 Sprinkle one color of glitter over the film, making sure all of the sticky surface is covered. Pat the glitter with your finger to ensure that it is firmly stuck.

Star Pendant Card

YOU WILL NEED

Star pendant

Pin

Card blank

Craft wire

Pencil

This is a good presentation technique for pendants, Christmas decorations, and other trinkets or mementos, as they can be removed and used by the recipient. For extra ornament, you could thread small beads onto the craft wire before you coil it.

1 Position the pendant on the card. Using a pin, pierce two holes in the front of the card, one through the hole in the pendant and the other just above the first one.

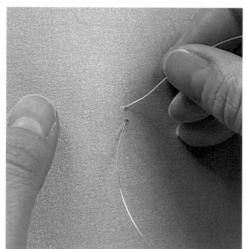

2 Cut approximately 20in (50cm) of craft wire. Working from the back of the card, poke one end of the wire through each hole.

3 Thread the pendant onto the lower piece of wire and push it right up to the card. Twist the wires tightly together.

4 | Wind one end of the wire around a pencil to make a coil. Slide the wire coil off the pencil. Repeat the process with the other end.

5 | Press the coils flat with your fingers.

Advent Calendar

YOU WILL NEED

Green card

Scissors

Craft knife

Silver pen

Christmas paper

Used greetings cards

Paper glue

Small red gift box

Ribbon rosette

This Advent calendar can be used every year at Christmas and provides the perfect way to recycle all those cards, pieces of gift wrap, and tags that people collect each year after the festive season. Have fun selecting your own 'windows' in your very own customized calender. If you want to make it even more personal, another idea is to use photographs of your friends and family instead.

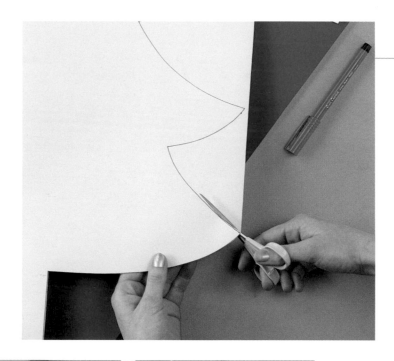

1 First make the Christmas tree pattern. Cut a piece of paper measuring about 25 x 20in (63 x 50cm) and fold in half lengthwise. Draw half the tree with a trunk against the foldline and cut it out. Open out flat and use the pattern as a template to cut out the tree in green card.

2 Cut a 1¼in (3cm) square of card to use as a template for the doors. Draw around the square twenty-three times on the back of the tree, positioning the doors at random but leaving the trunk clear. Cut three sides of the doors, leaving the right-hand side 'hinged' so the door opens the right way on the other side. On the right side of the tree, score the hinged side of each door lightly so it will open easily—but do not open the doors yet. Number the doors one to twenty-three with a silver pen.

3 Cut out small festive pictures from Christmas paper and used greetings cards. On the back of the tree, stick each picture behind a door by spreading paper glue on the tree around the doors.

5 Write the number twenty-four on the front of a small red gift box with a silver pen. Stick a ribbon rosette on the top and glue the box onto the tree trunk. Fill the box with candy. Stick a picture hanger on the back of the calendar at the top.

4 Decorate the calendar with a gold star on the top and circles of metallic card between the doors.

Gilded Bay Leaves

YOU WILL NEED

Bay leaves

Gold paint

Bronze or copper paint

Hot glue gun

Nuts or dried flowers

Whole bay leaves can either be gathered from a bush in your own garden, or that of a neighbor, or bought in a jar intended for culinary purposes from a supermarket. These gilded leaves make wrapped presents even more special.

1 Paint over both sides of the leaves with gold paint. To create different finishes, use several different golds or a bronze or copper color. Allow the leaves to dry on an old cake cooking rack.

2 Having wrapped up your parcel, attach the gilded leaves with a hot glue gun and add some nuts or dried flowers.

Woodland Tree Card

This traditional Christmas card is easily made from bracken that you can find at wintertime in forests and woodlands, or in your local florist.

1 | Cut a rectangle of white cardboard to measure 6½ x 2½in (16.5 x 6.5cm). Select a piece of bracken about 5½in (14cm) in length. Fix the bracken to the card with spots of glue on the underside. Leave sufficient space at the base of this 'tree' for the 'flower pot'. For the star, color a floret of fool's parsley gold, and glue to the tree. Cut a 8½ x 8in (21.5 x 20cm piece of card, crease and fold in half.

2 | Now draw a rectangle—larger than the white card—on the red card using a gold marker. Cut out a 'flower pot' from some red card, draw on some decorative lines and fix the pot to the tree. Cover the design card with protective film and fix it centrally within the gold border.

Christmas Potpourri Boxes

This is a simple but elegant way to use empty gift boxes as containers for potpourri. We have selected a green and a black box. For the potpourri you can use your own selection of fragrant items or follow the 'recipe' in step 2.

1 | Take the lid off one of the boxes and lightly secure three whole flower heads of cow parsley diagonally across it. With aerosol spray paint, give the top of the box two light coats of gold paint.

2 | When the paint is dry, remove the parsley to reveal the unsprayed part of the box. This shows up as a pretty pattern through the paint. Now fix the gold-sprayed cow parsley to the other box lid and repeat the process. These boxes are filled with a festive mixture of small cones, tree bark, and citrus peel. Cover the potpourri with plastic wrap before replacing the lids.

Patterned Paper and Gift Tags

YOU WILL NEED

Sheets of pale colored paper

Scrap paper

White candle

Purple, orange, and pink acrylic paint

Jam jar

Wide brush

There are so many ways in which to decorate paper. Here is one of the simplest methods. The pattern is created by drawing on the paper with a candle. When the paper is washed over with a strong color, the paint avoids areas where the wax has been applied, thus leaving a lighter area in the form of the pattern.

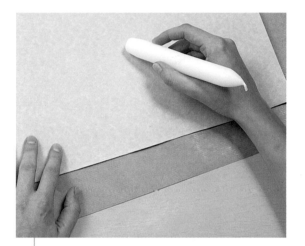

1 Lay the paper to be decorated on a smooth piece of scrap paper to protect the work surface. Draw your design on the paper by pressing really hard with the candle—this is easiest when the candle is cold.

2 Dilute the acrylic paint with water until it has the consistency of light cream. Brush the paint evenly across the surface of the paper to reveal the wax pattern. Lay the paper aside until the paint is dry.

3 Cut out simple shapes from the patterned paper and stick them onto pieces of contrasting-colored card to make co-ordinating tags. Here the card has been trimmed with pinking shears to make a decorative edge.

Christmas Bird Gift Tags

YOU WILL NEED

Colored origami paper

Template (see page 264)

Pencil

Small scissors

Scraps of colored hand-made thick paper

Paper glue

Chinese New Year 'money'

Pinking shears

Hole punch

Short lengths of narrow ribbon

It is extremely rewarding to make your own gift tags at Christmas and it is easy to create beautiful examples with the smallest scraps of paper left over from other projects. Success depends on combining materials with contrasting colors and interesting patterns. Brightly colored papercut designs, most often of elements from nature, are highly popular in Polish peasant art. You may also like to illustrate the theme from a traditional Christmas carol, such as 'The Twelve Days of Christmas.'

1 Draw around the bird template on a piece of pink origami paper and cut it out. Cut out a background slightly larger than the bird from colored hand-made paper. Stick the bird into the center with the paper glue and cut out freehand a crown and wings from the gold part of the Chinese 'money'. Stick in place.

2 Now cut a strip of the same paper the width of the card and trim the top edge with the pinking shears. Stick this along the bottom so it just covers the bird's feet.

3 Cut around the whole tag with pinking shears, keeping the bird centrally placed. Make a hole in one corner with the hole punch and thread with a pretty ribbon.

Christmas Gift Baskets

Basket-making is one of the most ancient and universal crafts. Although baskets were primarily made as purely functional objects, their materials, weaving patterns, and eventual shape mean that they are some of the most beautiful examples of human creativity and ingenuity.

YOU WILL NEED

Scrap paper (here sand-colored soft cotton rag paper and patterned wallpaper were used)

Small stapler

White glue

Small scissors

Paper clips

Mattress needle or needle with wide eye

Paper cord

Pinking shears

Two clothes pegs

1 | Cut seven strips of the plain scrap paper, each approximately 12in (30cm) long and ¾in (2cm) wide. Lay them down on the worksurface and weave together as shown, laying three strips across four to form the rectangular base of the basket.

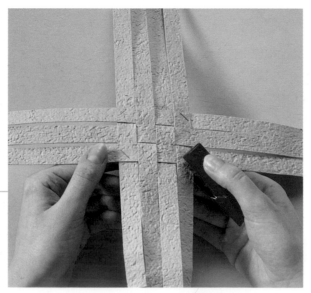

2 | Staple each of the four corners to hold the base firmly in place before building up the sides.

3 | Bend up all the strips to create the basic structure of the basket. Cut lengths from the patterned paper with the same measurements as before and weave the first layer alternately over and under the upright strips, gluing the beginning and end of each horizontal strip to hold it in place.

6 Use the needle to pierce holes in the woven section of the basket just below the rim and thread the paper cord through and over the rim. Finish off neatly and stick the end of the cord inside with white glue to secure.

4 Continue weaving until four layers are in place, then cut off the excess vertical strips using the small scissors.

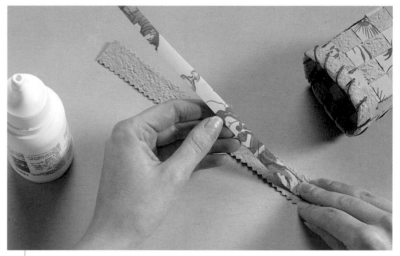

7 Cut a strip of the plain paper ¾in (2cm) wide and 8¾in (22cm) long. Cut each side with the pinking shears to make a pretty zigzagged edge. Stick a strip of the patterned paper ½in (1cm) wide along the center to make the handle.

5 Cut a length of the plain paper ¾in (2cm) wide and long enough to go around the rim of the basket with a small overlap. Fold it in half lengthways and fit over the rim as shown, holding temporarily in place with paper clips.

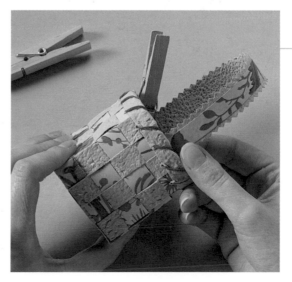

8 Glue each end inside the basket and hold in place with clothes pegs until the glue is completely dry and the handle firmly attached.

Glove Gift Tags

YOU WILL NEED

Templates (see page 265)

Hand-made ivory paper

Paper clips

Pencil

Small pointed scissors

Recycled pink paper

Pinking shears

Wad of tissue paper

Tracing wheel (in two sizes)

Craft knife

Cutting mat

Eraser

Paper glue

Length of ribbon

Hole punch

These subtle and elegant glove-shaped gift tags have been inspired by American folk art designs from the mid-nineteenth century. The heart was a favorite image used to symbolize enduring friendship. The hand or glove design is extremely apt to use as a gift tag due to its connotations of friendship and generosity.

1 Place the template on the ivory-colored paper and hold in place with paper clips. Draw around it with the pencil, remove the template, and cut around the glove shape with the small scissors

3 Place the glove shape on a wad of tissue paper to act as a yielding surface. Using the smaller tracing wheel, press firmly while wheeling it all around the edge of the glove. Make two parallel lines between each finger.

2 Fold the pink paper in half and place the straight side of the heart template against the fold. Cut out the heart plus the two curved strips, also using the template provided. Cut a zigzagged edge with the pinking shears along each edge of the strips.

4 Open up the pink heart and lay it on the glove with the point facing the cuff end. Lightly draw around it with a sharp pencil. Now cut four parallel v-shaped slits into the heart and in the heart shape on the back of the glove. Each arm of the slits should measure ½in (1cm).

5 Rub out the pencil marks on the glove. Take the heart, now with its pointed end facing the fingers, and carefully interlock the points of the corresponding slits. The heart is now securely fixed onto the glove.

6 Place the curved template onto the cuff of the back of the glove and draw two sets of parallel lines. Place the glove onto the cutting mat and cut twelve slits on the outer band between these lines and ten slits on the inner one.

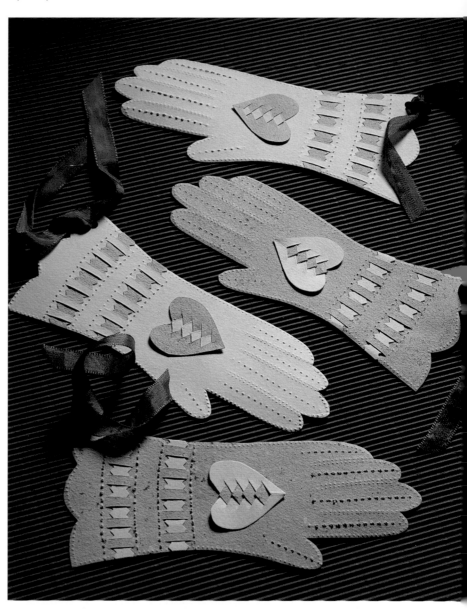

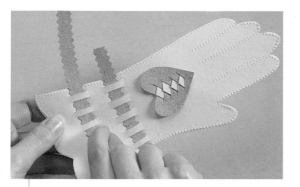

7 Turn the glove over to the right side and slot the pinked strips through the slits. Trim the ends so that ½in (1cm) overlaps, turn under to the back of the glove and stick down with paper glue.

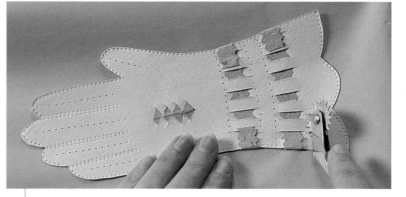

8 Still working from the wrong side, place the glove on the tissue paper and using the larger tracing wheel, mark each side of the strips on the cuff and along the centre of each finger and the thumb. To attach a ribbon, punch a hole at the edge of the cuff.

Crown Cards

YOU WILL NEED

❧

Metallic foil papers

❧

Template (see page 266)

❧

Pencil

❧

Scissors

❧

Wad of folded tissue paper

❧

Sewing tracing wheel

❧

Red card 12 x 8in
(30 x 20cm)

❧

Colored origami paper 4 x 6in
(10 x 15cm)

❧

Spray glue

These clever crowns have an 'embossed' design that can be created very easily, but looks very impressive. You can either use the design given on the template for this project or create your own crown motifs.

1 Cut out a piece of the metallic foil paper (handle it very carefully as it marks easily) and place the crown template onto the wrong side. Draw round it neatly with the pencil and cut out.

2 Still working on the back, mark the design on the foil paper with a pencil. Place the foil paper on the wad of folded tissue paper and roll the tracing wheel over the pencil guidelines. This will appear on the metallic side as raised dotted lines which catch the light beautifully.

3 Fold the red card carefully in half, scoring along the fold line. Using the spray glue, stick the red and orange origami paper very neatly in place, butting up to each other in the center of the card. Finally, spray the back of the crown design and stick centrally over the two-tone background.

Advent Tags

YOU WILL NEED

Template (see page 266)

Gold paper

Scissors

Scalpel

Red card

Pencil

Picture stickers

All-purpose adhesive

Sequins

Glitter pen

Gold string

The backing card for these tags is red but you could also use Christmas paper, as long as it is fairly stiff. You can hang these colorful tags on presents as an alternative to a card, or they can go on the boughs of a Christmas tree.

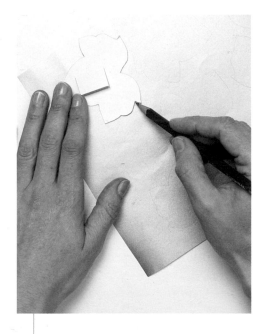

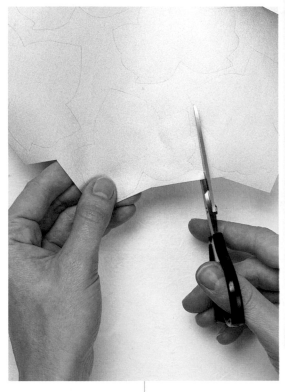

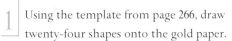

1 Using the template from page 266, draw twenty-four shapes onto the gold paper.

2 Roughly cut out the shapes so that you can tell approximately how large they will be when the tags are finished.

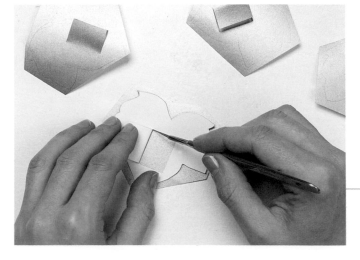

3 Using the scalpel and a template, on each tag cut out the door on three sides.

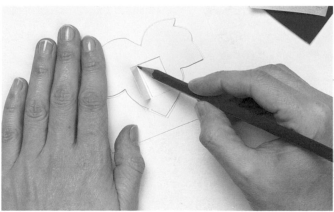

4 For the backs, draw around the template twenty-four times onto the red card and cut out roughly. On the reverse side of the card, mark where the doors are to go with the pencil and template.

Ivy Wreath

YOU WILL NEED

❦

6 long pieces of ivy

❦

Paintbrush

❦

Gold paint

❦

16in (40cm) of florist's wire

❦

Clear adhesive tape

❦

Gold spray paint

❦

6 chillies

❦

20 peanuts in their shells

❦

Thin gold cord

Richly colorful in red, green, and gold, this wreath will top the presents piled beneath the tree. Gather the ivy from nearby woods or a florist.

1 Paint the leaves of three of the pieces of ivy with gold paint. Leave to dry.

3 Spray the chillies and peanuts very lightly with gold paint. The original color should still show in places.

2 Make a 6in (15cm) circle using doubled florist's wire. Twist the ends around each other to secure. With clear tape, stick the pieces of ivy around the circle, one at a time, alternating gold and plain lengths.

4 With thin gold cord, tie the chillies by their stems and the peanuts around their middles to the wreath. Space them out and tie them on firmly.

❦

Three Kings Card

YOU WILL NEED

Template (see page 267)

Scissors

❦

Craft Knife

❦

Ruler

❦

Brocade

❦

Paper Glue

❦

Sequins

Once you have made your colorful figures for this card you can then use use them again as templates for decorating cards, tags or stencils. The three kings or 'three wise men' are a symbol of the approaching Christmas holiday so they make the perfect adornment for a card at this time.

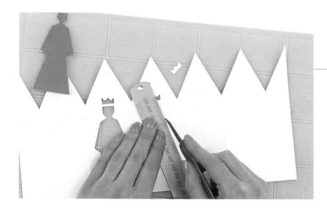

1 Cut gold card 12 x 6in (30 x 15cm) and score twice 3in (7.5cm) in from each side. Trace out the template and carefully work out where the points will fall. Mark the design on the back of the gold card and cut out using a sharp craft knife and ruler for straight edges.

2 Smooth the edges of the gold card with the back of your thumbnail if they have lifted. Cut the kings' clothes from three pieces of brocade, slightly larger than the apertures. Place small pieces of double-sided tape around the kings on the inside of the card and stick the brocade in place.

3 Cut the kings' gifts from gold card and glue in place. Attach sequins to points of their crowns. Stick on white card to cover the back of the center panel. To protect the points, slip a further piece of card into the envelope. The three kings which have been cut out could be used for a further card, gift tag, or stencil.

❦

Christmas Wreath Card

YOU WILL NEED

Glossy red card

Strips of colorful fabrics

Sewing machine

Embroidery thread

Gold pen

Double wool thread / Ribbon

There are a number of large wreaths you can make in this book—here is a mini-wreath for a card embellishment.

1 Cut glossy red card 7 x 9in (18 x 23cm), score and fold 4⅛in (11.5cm) across. Cut on the bias four strips of Christmas fabrics 1 x 12in (2.5 x 30cm) long. Fold strips lengthways, machine ⅛in (3mm) seam allowance. Leave length of thread at end, thread with bodkin.

3 Bind the ends with embroidery thread tie a knot and trim. Draw an arched border using a gold pen. Center the finished wreath and pierce through the card with a thick needle or point of dividers. Sew through the back, knot thread, trim and finish with glue.

2 Thread a length of double wool through each tube. Pin the ends of the tubes to a firm surface. Plait by laying four strands over the left hand, taking the left strand over two middle strands and the right strand over one. Continue to the end. Ease into a circle, cross over the ends and sew through to secure. Trim and finish with a bow.

Cathedral Windows

Cathedral windows are often used in quilt making and they add a real craft textile touch to a Christmas card. It is always nice to give a card that has the quality of a gift, however small the decoration.

1 Draw four 3½in (99cm) squares and cut out. Fold in ¼in (6mm) seam allowance and press. Find square center by folding diagonally each way and mark with iron tip. Fold down corner and pin. Continue with others to make a square. Catch centre points with a small stitch. Fold in again and sew.

3 Sew double squares together and place the third and fourth fir-tree patches over seams. Sew tiny beads in corners of 'windows'. Cut card 10 x 7in (25 x 18cm), score and fold 5in (12.5cm). Mark top centre and sides 2½in (6cm) down with pencil. Cut through card to form a point. Glue finished square centerd horizontally onto card. Add gold border.

2 Cut four ¾in (2cm) squares from fir-tree fabric. Place two red squares right sides together and sew down one side to make double square. Pin fir-tree patch diagonally over seam on right side and curl back folded edges surrounding patch. Slip stitch to hold in place. Repeat to make 1 more.

Christmas Stocking Card

YOU WILL NEED

❦

Template (see page 267)

❦

Silver pen

❦

Red felt

❦

Water soluble pen

❦

Scissors

❦

Felt tip pens

❦

Sequin waste

Sequin waste is a very useful craft material and is used here to make stockings for cards on which any small gifts can be fixed. In this example a small eraser has been used, but you could also attach candies in colorful wrappers or perhaps a small photograph.

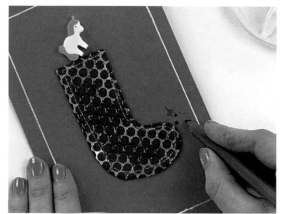

1 Cut card 7 x 9in (18 x 23cm). Score and fold 4½in (11.5cm). Draw border in silver pen around card. Trace the template and transfer onto thin card. Draw round template onto red felt using a water-soluble pen. It is not easy to mark sequin waste so hold the template in place and cut round it.

3 Glue the stocking to card, then add the little pony eraser or another small gift that can be glued on. Draw holly and berries using felt pens. You could also add beads and sequins if you wish.

2 Sew the sequin waste to felt by hand or machine, then trim both layers neatly.

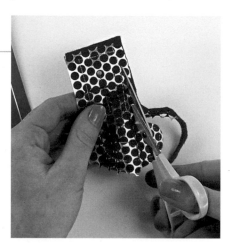

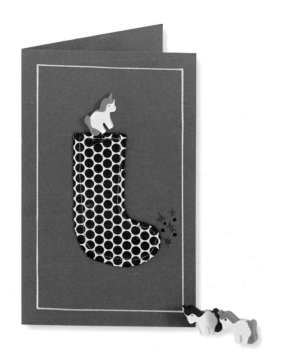

Candlelit Tree

YOU WILL NEED

Green card

Template (see page 267)

Tracing paper

Sewing machine

Self-adhesive spots

Narrow satin ribbon

All-purpose adhesive

Tweezers

Scissors

This attractive tree card could also be used as a decoration in its own right. Simply punch a hole though the top of the tree beneath the gold star and thread some strong nylon thread through in a loop to hang from your tree.

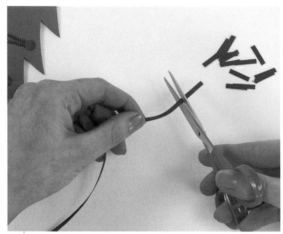

1 Cut card 6 x 8in (15 x 20cm) and score down center. Trace template and transfer onto thin card and draw round on green card. Cut out using craft knife. Set your sewing machine to a fairly wide satin stitch.

3 Glue the ribbon pieces in place at the end of branches on the back of the card. Tweezers will help you to hold them steady. Leave until the glue dries. Cut the tops diagonally to look like candles. Add a red star on top of the tree.

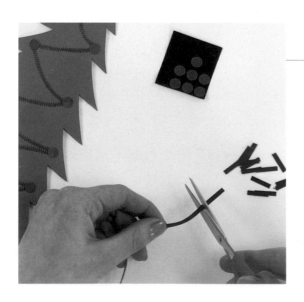

2 Stick on self-adhesive spots to resemble Christmas tree baubles. Cut narrow satin ribbon into fourteen ½in (1cm) pieces.

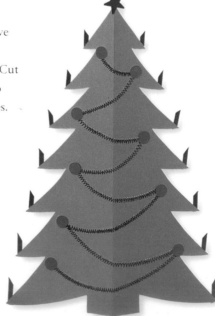

The Friendly Snowman Card

The snowman at the window invites us to come outside to play in the snow. This is such a pretty card, why not decorate it with surrounding 'drifts' of absorbent cotton balls displayed somewhere where your card can be seen?

YOU WILL NEED

❧

Colored card

❧

Piece of film

❧

Paper

❧

Pencil

❧

Chinagraph pencils

❧

Silver pen

❧

Double-sided tape

1 | Cut off left hand side of this card so that light will shine through window. Cut a piece of film slightly smaller than folded card. Draw snowman and trees on to the paper Place paper under film and on right side draw outline of snowman and trees.

3 | Turn back the film onto the right side and draw in the scarf and nose with a red chinagraph pencil. Add face details in silver. Attach the film to the inside of card with double-sided tape and place a silver star where it can be seen shining through window.

2 | Turn over the film and color in the trees and snowman using a white chinagraph pencil.

❧

A Christmas Fir Tree Card

YOU WILL NEED

White card

Green plastic strips

Orange and yellow tissue paper

Self-adhesive

Spray glue

Steel ruler

Sharp craft knife

This is a simple, easily-made card in unusual colors for Christmas. You can recycle old colorful plastic bags for this project as these make a durable material with an interesting texture.

1 Cut card 4¼ x 8in (11 x 20cm), score and fold 4in (10cm). The fold is at the top of card. Cut a strip of green plastic from an old shopping bag. Tear four strips of tissue in shades of orange and yellow. The fir-tree is from a strip of self-adhesive 'stickers'.

3 Trim excess paper from the edges of the card with a steel ruler and sharp craft knife.

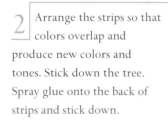

2 Arrange the strips so that colors overlap and produce new colors and tones. Stick down the tree. Spray glue onto the back of strips and stick down.

Paper Holly Christmas Card

YOU WILL NEED

Silver card

Template (see page 268)

Thin card for templates

Dark and light-green satin paper

Spray glue

Self-adhesive red spots

The silver card shows off the greens and reds of the holly to stunning effect in this simple design. You will need to buy some satin paper from a craft shop to use for the glossy leaves.

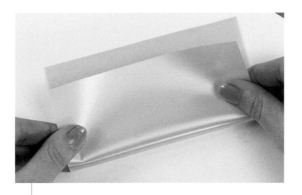

1 Cut silver card 12 x 6in (30 x 15cm), score and fold 6in (15cm). Trace templates and transfer onto card.

2 Cut 5in (13cm) square of satin paper and 4in (10cm) square of dark green tissue-paper. Fold these squares in half twice, then diagonally across to make a triangle. Cut out larger holly from satin paper and unfold, then dark green holly. You can draw round templates first if you find it easier.

3 Spray glue onto the backs of holly leaves. Position the larger, pale-green leaves first, then the dark green on top, between the pale-green leaves. Stationer's self-adhesive spots make red berries. Put on five or so.

Curled Ribbon Tree Card

YOU WILL NEED

Silver or gold card

Pencil

Sequin waste

All-purpose adhesive

Narrow ribbon

Card or paper for base

Sequin star

This clever card is made using sequin waste and colorful ribbons in a truly ingenious way. This would also make a good wedding or christening card as the curled ribbons add a celebratory touch—you can simply cut out appropriate shapes for the occasion and thread the ribbons through.

1 | Cut card 6 x 8½in (15 x 22cm), score and fold 4¼in (11cm) along the top. Mark center top of the card with the pencil dot. Cut the triangle from sequin waste, place on the card and mark two sides at the bottom of the tree. Glue along edges of tree and hold in place on card until the glue dries. Any residue glue can be rubbed away when it is dry.

2 | Cut a base for the tree from a piece of card or paper. Curl over scissors a number of narrow pieces of ribbon cut about 3¾in (9.5cm) long.

3 | Glue on base and add sequin star to top of tree. Slip curled ribbons through every other hole in sequin waste and every other row, starting at top of tree. There is no need to tie them; they will stay in place.

New Year Dove Card

This dove of peace for New Year is made from a paper doily with calendar dates falling from its beak. Once the festivities are over and you find yourself looking forward to a new year, send this card to friends and congratulate them on surviving Christmas!

1 | Cut deep blue card 12 x 8in (30 x 20cm), score 6in (15cm) and fold. Draw freehand two curves at the top of the card to represent clouds and cut with a craft knife.

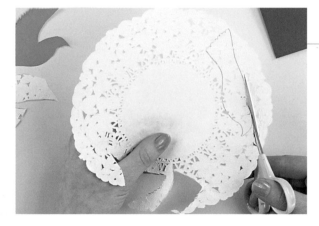

2 | Trace the dove template and transfer to thin card to make your own template. Trace out the dove onto white paper doily and cut out, together with dates 1 and 31 from an old calendar and the strip of translucent film waved along the upper edge to resemble hills

3 | Spray glue all pieces and place on the card with with four star sequins. Using a silver pen, draw a line along the edge of cloud curves.

Scottish New Year Card

New Year celebrations are particularly associated with Scotland. So here, in traditional Scottish style, we have plaid and golden bells for our New Year greeting. These bell templates could also be used to make 2-dimensional tree decorations.

YOU WILL NEED

Ready-cut window card

Craft knife

Ruler

Plaid fabric or paper

Spray glue

Gold card

Tracing paper template (see page 268)

Small scissors

Narrow satin ribbon

1 With a sharp craft knife and ruler, remove the left-hand section of the three-fold ready-cut window card. Use this spare card to make two bells.

2 Cut a piece of tartan fabric or paper to fit inside back of card, attach with spray glue and trim edges. Trace template and transfer on to spare gold card. Cut out and back with plaid using spray glue. Trim with small scissors. Punch holes in bells.

3 Make a bow from narrow satin ribbon and cut a length for the bells to hang from. Thread the first bell and hold in place with a dab of glue. Thread second bell. Sew through the bow and ends of the bell's ribbon to hold in place, glue at top of circular window, so that the bells hang free.

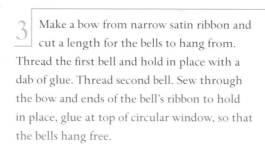

Potato Print Gift wrap

YOU WILL NEED

❧

1 large potato

❧

Sharp or craft knife

❧

Pencil

❧

Plain paper

❧

Poster paint

❧

Paintbrush

Employ a humble potato to create simple yet beautiful designs. Begin by cutting a large potato in half and draw a simple design on it. A cross motif has been used here but you could also use the heart, star, and tree templates in this book.

1 | Use a sharp knife or craft knife to sculpt the potato, leaving the design raised from the surface.

2 | To ensure a regular print, draw a grid lightly in pencil on a sheet of plain paper. Then mix up fairly thick poster paint and apply it to the potato-cut with a paintbrush. Print the design in the middle of each square of the grid. You should be able to do two or three prints before the color fades and needs replenishing.

3 | Cover the whole sheet with one design. Cut another design on another potato half; repeat the whole process, this time printing on the cross of the grid. When the paint is thoroughly dry, rub out the grid lines still visible and wrap up your present.

Holly Gift Decoration

YOU WILL NEED

Plain paper

Pencil

Green card

Absorbent cotton

Red tissue paper

All-purpose adhesive

Double-sided tape

Holly leaves are an attractive shape and perfect for decorating a festive gift. If you can not find any real holly you could also make this project to decorate your home; as a centrepiece for your table, or to go on a mantlepiece or coffee table with some scented candles.

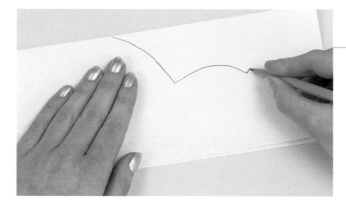

1 Measure the length of the diagonal across the top of your parcel. On a sheet of plain paper, draw a large holly leaf, the 'vein' of which measures slightly more than half the length of the diagonal.

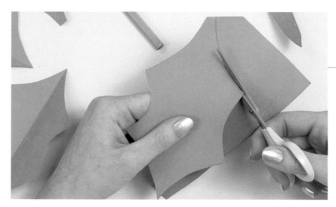

2 Trace four holly leaves onto some green card, using the template you have just created. Cut the leaves out and bend them in the middle; creasing them slightly where the central vein would be.

3 Make the berries from a ball of absorbent cotton wrapped in two squares of red tissue paper. Put a dab of glue inside and twist up the tissue tightly at the base. When the glue is dry, cut off as much excess twist as possible. Group the leaves and berries on the parcel; attach with glue or double-sided tape.

Christmas Bells Decoration

These Christmas bells will ring out gaily from your present. If you want to decorate them further you can attach beads, sequins or even candy wrappers to add a touch of color.

1 | Cut out the two bell-shaped templates, with one showing the outline of the clapper from the bottom edge. From thin card, cut out two of each shape.

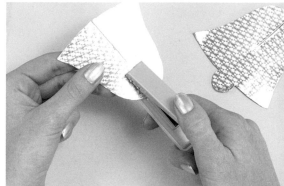

3 | Pierce a hole in the top of the plain bell shapes and thread them with a length of ribbon. Then slot the pairs of bell shapes together (i.e. the plain one, and the one with the clapper) so that they form three-dimensional shapes, as shown here. Tie a group of as many bells as you like onto your gift. This idea can also be used for decorating a wedding gift.

2 | Cover all the card shapes with gold paper (or any color which would co-ordinate with your Christmas paper). Cover both sides, and trim away all the excess paper. On the bell shapes with the clapper, cut a slit from the curved top of the bell to the center of the bell. On the others (the plain ones) cut a slit from the middle of the bottom edge, also to the center.

209

Christmas Bottle Wrap

YOU WILL NEED

Thin-red card

Pencil

Ruler

Craft knife

Absorbent cotton

All-purpose adhesive

Bottles of seasonal spirits make an ideal present—but hide such an obvious-looking gift under the decorative guise of a Christmas tree. Find a flower-pot just big enough to take the base of the bottle.

1 | Find a flower-pot just big enough to take the base of the bottle. From thin card cut out a third section of a large circle and make a deep cone about 3in (8cm) shorter than the bottle. Cover the cone with suitable paper.

2 | Put the bottle in the flower-pot and place the cone on top. You may need to trim the cone if it seems to cover too much of the flower-pot; do this with care, since you could easily make the cone too short! Double over a piece of tinsel, tie it in a knot, and stick it on top of the 'tree'.

Snowman Gift Cover

What fun for a child to see Frosty and know that the snowman's hiding a gift! In this project you need to wrap up a cylindrical gift in paper to form the body of the snowman. Then you can have lots of fun decorating him with features, a scarf, and even a little hat. This would make a good project for small children who might like to decorate their sibling's presents.

YOU WILL NEED

Paper

Newspaper

Absorbent cotton

All-purpose adhesive

Adhesive tape

Black poster paint

Red and patterned ribbon

1 Wrap up a cylindrical gift in paper to form the body of the snowman. Crush newspaper into a shape for the head and stick it on top of the gift. Cover the body with absorbent cotton, sticking it on with dabs of glue. Create a face from bits of paper and stick in place.

2 For the hat, you need a strip of card, plus a circle big enough to make the brim. Draw an inner circle in the brim, the diameter of Frosty's head; cut it out to form the 'lid' of the hat. Roll the strip of card up to form the crown of the hat; stick it in place with tape.

3 Stick on the top of the hat, then attach the brim, putting strips of tape inside the crown. Paint the hat with black poster paint; it'll need two or three coats. Wrap around the red ribbon to form a cheery hat-band and put it on Frosty's head. Fray the ends of some patterned ribbon to form a scarf and tie it firmly in place.

Jolly Santa Gift Tag

YOU WILL NEED

Thin red card

Pencil

Ruler

Craft Knife

Absorbent cotton

All-purpose adhesive

Hole punch

A three-dimensional Santa Claus tag, complete with fluffy beard, provides a jolly festive decoration on a gift. This would make another good project for children, but make sure that they get help from an adult when cutting out shapes with sharp scissors!

1 Draw a fairly large rectangle on thin red card; make sure that all the corners are right angles. Score down the middle and fold the card, creasing it well. Draw an inverted 'V' for Santa's hat, and a curve for his chin; cut them out with a craft knife.

2 Curve the hat and chin outward to give them a three-dimensional look, then draw in the eyes and mouth. Form a beard from a small piece of absorbent cotton, and stick it in position with a dab of glue. Do the same with the fur trim on the edge of the hat and the pom-pom on its tip. Punch a hole in the back of the label, write your message, and tie the tag on the parcel.

Festive Frills Gift Decoration

Why not decorate your Christmas present as if it were a Christmas tree—with glittering baubles and tinsel? It's a great way to use up left-over decorations and will certainly make your presents a little bit different.

YOU WILL NEED

Christmas paper

Baubles

Tinsel

Double-sided tape

1 Wrap the gift in some elegant paper; something plain but shiny will set off the baubles better than a more complex Christmas design—you could use foil or paper. Then thread Christmas baubles onto a length of tinsel.

2 Decide where you want to put the decoration and cover the area with a few strips of double-sided tape. If the parcel is rectangular, put the baubles in one corner; if the parcel is square, the middle would be better. An upright parcel like that shown here looks best with the decoration on the top. Group the baubles into a bunch on the gift, wrapping the tinsel around them to form a nest.

Angel's Message Gift Tag

A heavenly messenger bears good greetings on this Christmas present. Once you have made the figure you can also place her in your home—the little angel may like perching on the top of your Christmas tree!

1 Cut a quarter section of a circle from light card to form a narrow cone for the body. On a folded piece of paper draw one arm and one wing against the edge of the fold as shown, so that when they are cut out you will have a pair of each.

2 Make the cone and cover it with silver paper (aluminium foil would do). Trace the arm and wings on to silver paper; cut them out and glue them in their relevant positions on the body.

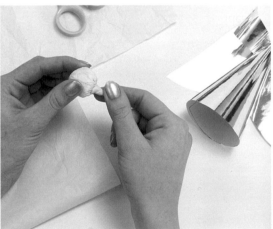

3 Make the head by rolling up some white tissue paper into a firm ball, twisting the ends of the tissue tightly to form a 'neck'. Glue the head into the top of the cone. Tie a scrap of tinsel into a loose knot and stick it on the head as a halo. Make a scroll from white paper, write on your message and stick it between the angel's hands. Attach the angel to the gift with double-sided tape.

Stocking Tags

Pencil

Thin card

Bright paper

Plain paper

Light card

Paper glue

Hole punch

With so many presents being exchanged at this time of the year, tags become even more important. What about some special stocking ones? Use the template in the book or create your own designs if you prefer.

2 Trace around the template onto thin card and then cut out the shape and cover it with bright paper; try to co-ordinate the colors and themes with those in the gift wrap you use for your present.

3 Cut around the outline and punch a hole at the top of the tag. Write your message and tie the tag on to the parcel. You could cheat a little when designing the shape of your tag by tracing an illustration from a magazine or by using the outline of a pastry cutter.

1 Choose any festive shape such as the stocking shown here. To ensure that your design is symmetrical, fold a piece of paper in half and draw on half the design against the fold. Cut around the outline through both layers of paper; open out and use this as a template for the design.

Gifts *and* Food

Silver Pendant

Similar in texture and feel to polymer clay, precious metal clay is wonderful stuff. It contains pure silver, and when you heat it, the carrying medium is burned away and you are left with a piece of silver. This clay can be bought in kit form with the butane torch, fireproof block, wire brush, and full instructions.

1 Lay the playing card on a flat surface and rub a little vegetable oil onto it to stop the clay sticking. Position a piece of plastic on either side of it; these will act as depth guides when you are rolling out the clay.

2 Roll out the clay so the pin touches the plastic guides.

3 Stamp into the clay, pressing gently.

4 | Using the craft knife, cut out the pendant.

5 | Use the pointed tool to make a hole to hang the pendant from. Leave it to dry.

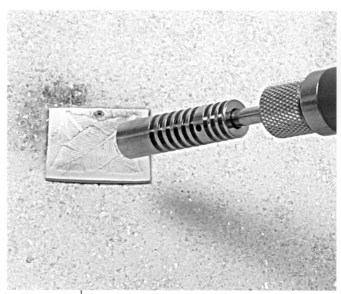

6 | Following the manufacturer's instructions, carefully place the pendant on the fireproof block and heat it until it glows. Leave it to cool completely.

7 | Use the wire brush to remove the white residue on the surface of the pendant, revealing the shining silver.

Jelly Wax Candle

YOU WILL NEED

Jelly wax

Wick

Glass container

Selection of stones and shells

This amazing transparent jelly can be used alone, with inclusions, or in combination with other waxes. Using jelly wax chunks as inclusions in a candle molded in either beeswax or paraffin wax produces a remarkable, vibrant mosaic effect.

1 Melt the wax together with any color in a double boiler, to 203°F (95°C). You may find it easier to place it in an oven instead. Do not let any water splash into the wax or it will turn cloudy. Concentrated pigments may be available for use with jelly wax, and should be added to the melted wax in a proportion of 0.1–0.2 per cent. You can also get predyed wax that can be added to melted plain jelly wax.

2 Support the wick and pour a little wax into the bottom of the container to hold the inclusions steady. Allow this to set, reposition any inclusions that have moved, then refill to ¾in (2cm) below the rim. Pour slowly to avoid creating too many bubbles. In larger candles, pour the wax in layers, inserting additional inclusions once each layer has cooled. For the candle shown here, retain a little wax, remove it from the heat, and allow it to set.

3 Add pieces of spare wax on the top of the candle, ensuring the wick has room to breathe.

Amaretto Wrappers

YOU WILL NEED

Template (see page 269)

Stencil card cut to the size of the
finished wrappers

Pencil

Scalpel or craft knife

Cutting mat

Tissue paper

Pebbles

Gold spray paint

Rough paper

Organza ribbon

If the tissue paper ends up being slightly larger than the stencil, don't worry: it will have a lovely golden edge in addition to the golden stencil.

1 Using the templates on page 269 or one of your own (perhaps copy a design from a Christmas card or paper), transfer the design onto stencil card. Simple geometric designs work best.

3 Cut pieces of tissue paper to the same size as the card. Lay the card over the tissue paper, on rough paper to protect your worksurface, and use pebbles to hold it in place. Lightly spray with gold spray paint.

2 On a cutting mat, carefully cut out the design with the scalpel or craft knife.

4 When the paint is dry, wrap each biscuit or sweet in a stenciled paper and tie the ends with organza ribbon.

Snowflake Sewing Box

Almost everyone's experience of papercutting goes back to childhood and making simple snowflakes cut with scissors from a circle of white paper at Christmas-time. These were often displayed in classroom windows. They remain some of the most beautiful and satisfying objects to make from cut paper.

1 Cut out a circle of the paper 12in (30cm) in diameter or the same size as the lid of the box (it is easiest to place the lid on the paper and draw around it). Fold paper four times to make eight sections, then fold each quarter back on itself.

3 Lay the marked and folded paper on the cutting mat and use the craft knife to cut away the areas indicated. You will need to press firmly for the knife to cut through all the layers. If you find this too difficult to do all at once, cut a few layers at a time.

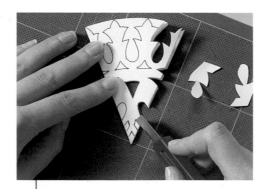

2 Lay the template on the folded circle and hold in place with paper clips. Draw carefully around the shape with the pen to transfer the design ready for cutting.

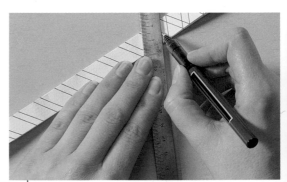

4 Cut a strip of the paper long enough to go round the side of the box and 2⅓in (6cm) deep. Fold into four lengthways, concertina-style, and mark a series of parallel lines along it at regular angles with the pen and the metal ruler.

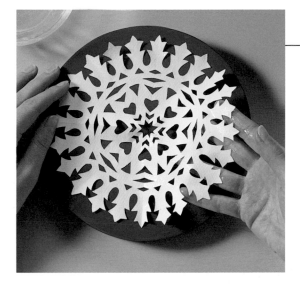

7 Open out the snowflake and smear with paste on both sides, as with the trellis strip. Place carefully on the center of the lid and smooth with your fingers to release any excess paste or air bubbles. Allow the paste to dry overnight, then paint with two coats of protective acrylic varnish.

5 Place the strip on the cutting mat and cut away these triangles on either side using the craft knife. At this stage you need to be careful and accurate, so take your time.

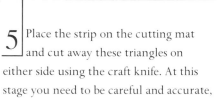

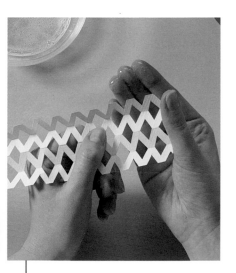

6 When you have finished cutting, open out the strip to reveal the even trellis pattern. Mix up the wallpaper paste according to the instructions and smear a thin layer on both sides of the paper. Stick in place around the side of the box and smooth with your fingers to expel any surplus glue or air bubbles. Trim to match at the join.

Fern-Patterned Vase

YOU WILL NEED

10in (25cm) tall clear glass vase

Methylated spirits

Pressed leaves or ferns

Spray mount

Glass etching spray

Real etched glass requires considerable skill and a great deal of patience, but there is a far quicker and easier way to create a similar effect with nothing more than an aerosol can of etching spray, spray mount, and some pressed leaves. Ferns have been used for this vase, but any leaf with a clearly defined outline can be used.

1 Wash the vase thoroughly, dry and wipe the surface with methylated spirits to ensure good adhesion of the etching spray.

3 Spray the vase with etching spray, following the manufacturer's instructions for the best results. You will get a better finish if you apply three thin coats rather than one heavy one. Allow five minutes drying time between applications.

2 In a well ventilated room, spray the top side of the fern leaves with spray mount and carefully position them on the vase, pressing each frond in place.

4 Leave to dry fully for one hour and then peel off the fern leaves. Gently wash off any small pieces of leaf which get left behind. Vases decorated in this way can be hand-washed, but should not be placed in a dishwasher.

Aniseed Cookies

YOU WILL NEED

INGREDIENTS

4 eggs

*1lb 1½oz (500g) confectioner's
sugar*

1lb 1½oz (500g) white flour

2 dessertspoons (20ml) aniseed

EQUIPMENT

Baking tray

Rolling pin

Cookie molds

Sharp knife

Aniseed cookies are traditionally baked at Christmas in Switzerland and Germany, where exquisite examples can be bought from good bakers' shops. They are often given as presents and, rather than being eaten, are hung on the wall as decorations.

1 Beat the eggs together with the confectioner's sugar until light and fluffy, using an electric whisk if you have one. Mix in the flour and gradually add the aniseed. Turn out the mixture onto a lightly floured surface and knead very lightly. Roll out the dough to a thickness of approximately ½in (1cm).

2 Lay the mold gently on the dough and, without pressing, cut around the mold to release a piece of dough the same size as the mould.

3 Press the mould firmly and evenly down onto the dough to transfer the image. Lift off carefully and place the biscuit on a very lightly greased baking tray.

4 Using the larger composite mold, press firmly and evenly onto the pastry. Remove the mold and cut the resulting images up into smaller cookies. Place these on the lightly greased baking tray and, most importantly, leave to dry overnight. Bake low down in an oven preheated to 140°C/275°F/gas 1 for approximately 35 minutes or until cookies have risen.

Gingerbread House

YOU WILL NEED

INGREDIENTS

4oz (100g) butter

7oz (200g) black treacle

6oz (175g) honey

1lb 1½oz (500g) all-purpose white flour

4oz (100g) ground almonds

1 tbsp (15ml) ground ginger

1 tsp (5ml) mixed spice

1 tsp (5ml) cinnamon

½ tsp (2.5ml) nutmeg

2 tsp (10ml) bicarbonate of soda

4oz (100g) chopped preserved ginger

4oz (100g) chopped mixed peel

You will need to make 3 times this amount for the house shown here.

ROYAL ICING

1lb 1½oz (500g) confectioner's sugar

Whites of 2 large eggs

1 tsp (5ml) lemon juice

EQUIPMENT

Rolling pin

2 baking trays

Templates (see pages 271–273)

Small kitchen knife

Piping bag and nozzles

Cake board 9 x 13in (23 x 33cm)

This is an elegant adaptation of the more homely German tradition of making a Lebkuchen Haus at Christmas. These confectionery masterpieces were generally more in the style of a Hansel and Gretel-type cottage, freely decorated with drifts of icing snow and lavishly adorned with brightly colored sweets and enticing cookies.

1 Warm the butter, treacle, and honey in a pan until blended, then cool a little. In a bowl mix together the dry ingredients, chopped ginger, and peel. Add the cooled butter mixture to the dry ingredients. Mix together, turn onto a floured surface and knead lightly. Add a little milk if the dough is too dry or a little flour if too wet. Roll out onto the greased baking tray to a thickness of ⅜in (1cm).

2 Lay the template on the pastry and cut around it. Repeat for the sides and roof pieces. The back is cut from the front template without cutting out the windows and door. Preheat the oven to 400°F/200°C/gas 6 and bake for about 20 minutes until a rich brown color. Allow to cool, then remove from the tray. If the gingerbread has spread, replace the template and cut around once more.

3 | Beat the egg whites until frothy and slowly add the sifted sugar and lemon juice, beating until it holds up in peaks. Fill the icing bag and use the smallest nozzle to pipe around the windows and door. Pipe a double line around the front and fill in with dots. Pipe a border along the bottom and add dots and stars. Decorate the sides as shown.

4 | Pipe the design onto the roof pieces—a crossed border along the top with a latticework design on the main section. To finish, pipe a dot into each diamond. The back of the house need not be decorated as it will not be seen.

5 | To make the icing glue, beat the remaining royal icing mixture until it becomes much thicker. Fill the piping bag and insert a larger nozzle. Pipe a generous amount of the icing along the size and back of the cake board. Pipe another line up the side of the back wall where it will join the side wall. Place the back and side on the icing glue and push the side against the back, making sure that they both stand upright.

6 | Continue in this manner adding the other side and front. The icing glue is very strong and should hold the pieces together well when it sets. Pipe along the top of the roof and along the front edges of the gable end. Carefully put the front section of the roof on the house and press it gently into place. Repeat to attach the back section.

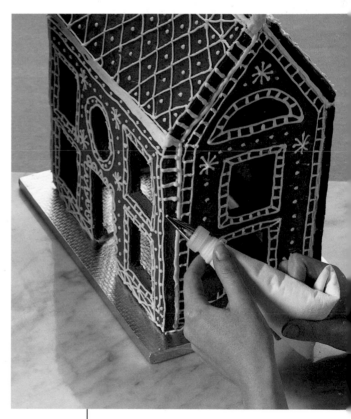

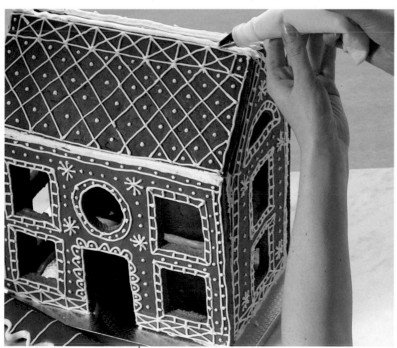

7 | When the two roof sections are in place, a small gap will be left between them at the top. Pipe along both edges of this gap and fix the roof ridge in place.

8 | Clean away any icing glue that oozes out of the joins from under the base of the house with the kitchen knife. Replace the narrow nozzle on the bag and, using the original icing mixture, disguise the joins by piping into them as well as piping horizontal lines up the sides, the front, and roof.

Chocolate Snowflake Stars

YOU WILL NEED

INGREDIENTS

7oz (200g) dark chocolate

8oz (225g) butter, softened

8oz (225g) fine granulated sugar

3 eggs

Pinch of salt

1lb 1½oz (500g) flour

ROYAL ICING

*1lb 1½oz (500g) confectioner's
sugar*

Whites of 2 large eggs

1 tsp (5ml) lemon juice

EQUIPMENT

Rolling pin

Baking tray

Star-shaped cookie cutter

Icing bag and nozzle

Simple to make and decorated using the enduring wintry theme of snowflakes, these delicious star-shaped cookies will appeal to children—in fact they could be made by children who love to stamp out interesting shapes with tin cookie cutters. These can be found in many different shapes and sizes in good kitchen supply stores.

1 Melt the chocolate, add to the softened butter and mix. In another bowl beat the sugar and eggs together, add a pinch of salt and the flour. Stir in the chocolate mixture. Turn out onto a floured surface and knead lightly, then roll out the pastry to a thickness of 5mm (2⅛in).

3 Sift the confectioner's sugar. Beat the egg whites until just frothy and slowly add the sifted sugar and the lemon juice, beating all the time until the icing stands up in peaks. Fill the icing bag and, using the finest nozzle, pipe a star shape onto the cookies. The icing must be just the right consistency to make good clean lines—if it is too runny it will spread; too stiff and it will not adhere to the cookie when set.

2 Cut out the star shapes with the cookie cutter and place them carefully on a baking tray. Preheat the oven to 400°F/200°C/gas 6 and bake for 10 minutes. Remove from oven, and allow to cool.

4 Now pipe radiating lines from the simple star shape to form a snowflake. When the icing has set, store in an airtight tin.

Meringue Mice

YOU WILL NEED

*4 egg whites
(at room temperature)*

*8oz (225g)
fine granulated sugar*

Baking tray

Waxproof paper

Piping bag

Palette knife

Edible silver balls

Peppercorns

Split almonds

Bradawl

Gold wire string

PREPARATION

*Place the egg whites
in a large bowl and whisk at high
speed until soft peaks form. Add
the sugar, 1 tsp at a
time, whisking well
each time.*

Meringue is best cooked at a low temperature for two hours so make sure you have plenty of time ahead of you. This recipe makes about sixteen mice.

1 | Line the baking tray with waxproof paper and heat the oven to 225°F/100°C/gas ¼. Then spoon the mixture into a piping bag and squeeze wedge shapes on the waxproof paper.

2 | Smooth the shapes into small mice-like bodies using the palette knife. Keep back some of the meringue for step 4.

3 | To make the mice faces, add silver balls for the noses, peppercorns for the eyes (don't forget to remove these before eating!), and split almonds for the ears.

4 Bake in the oven for about two hours or until very slightly golden. Cool and then use the bradawl to poke a small hole for the tail. Add the gold wire string for the tail, fastening it with uncooked meringue.

Festive Cookies

YOU WILL NEED

4oz (110g) butter

2oz (50g) fine granulated sugar

Grated rind of one lemon

5oz (150g) all-purpose flour

Rolling pin

Variety of cutters

Wax paper

Baking tray

Edible silver balls

Bradawl

Silver string

Edible silver balls are very attractive decorations and can be used for all sorts of patterns and pictures on these pretty cookies.

1 Mix all the ingredients together in a mixer. Heat the oven to 240°F/180°C/gas 4 and roll out the pastry on a floured surface.

2 Cut out a variety of shapes using the cookie cutters. Try to cut as many as possible from the pastry so that you don't have to roll it out too frequently.

3 Lay the cookies on a piece of waxproof paper on a baking tray and decorate with the edible silver balls.

4 | Make a hole in each
cookie with the bradawl
before putting them in the
oven for 10 minutes until pale
brown. Once cooked, cool on
a wire rack, and thread the
holes with silver string
to hang.

Christmas Tree Cake

YOU WILL NEED

Tree-shaped Christmas cake

Ready-to-roll icing

Green food coloring

Confectioner's sugar

Edible cale balls

Red ribbon bows

Glass-headed beads

Tree decoration 'presents'

Red wax candles

This festive Christmas tree cake will be the featured attraction at a Christmas tea. The cake can be made to your own traditional recipe and should be baked in a Christmas tree cake tin.

1 The simplest method for icing the cake is to use read-to-roll fondant icing. Knead the block into a ball and work in some green food coloring.

2 Roll the colored icing out flat on a cool surface, first sprinkling some confectioner's sugar on the worktop to prevent the icing from sticking.

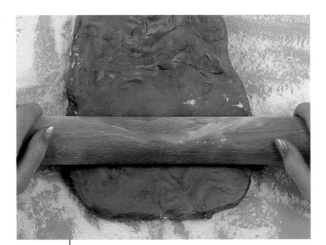

3 Carefully roll the sheet of icing over the rolling pin and unroll it onto the cake. Shape the icing around the cake, keeping your hands wet to smooth out any cracks.

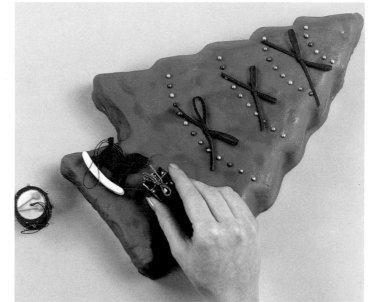

4 | Add rows of edible cake balls to suggest garlands draped across the tree.

6 | Place a selection of 'presents' around the bottom of the tree—the ones used here are Christmas tree decorations.

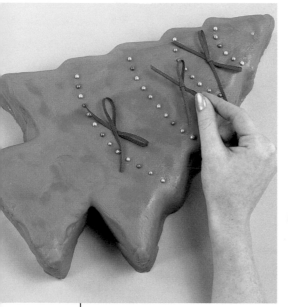

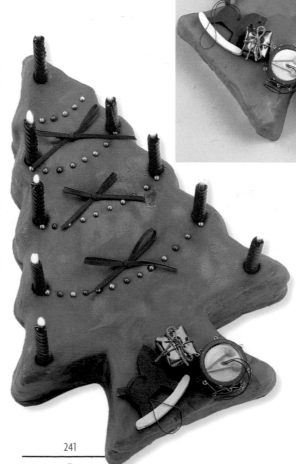

7 | Push red wax candles into the icing around the edges of the tree to complete the effect.

5 | Place tiny red ribbon bows on the cake. (You can use a glass-headed pin to secure the bows, but take care to remove them all before serving the cake.)

Christmas Tree Treats

YOU WILL NEED

Variety of cutters

Greased baking sheet

Confectioner's sugar

Water

Waxed thread or ribbon

These edible decorations are ideal for children to make and give to their friends or teachers. Make the cookies following a basic recipe using sugar, eggs, flour, and butter in the usual proportions. Alternatively, you can also use the recipe featured on page 238.

1 | Cut the dough into festive shapes. Skewer a hole in each, so that you can push a thread through later. (This may close up during baking—in which case you will have to pierce another hole in them when they are cold—but very carefully, as the biscuits have a habit of breaking!) Put them onto a greased baking sheet, and bake them at 350°F/180°C/gas 4, for 15 minutes.

2 | When the cookies are cool, make up some fairly stiff icing using confectioner's sugar and water, and ice them. Thread them onto some waxed thread—or ribbon if the hole is big enough.

Almond Bunches

YOU WILL NEED

For each bunch:

*2 4in (10cm) squares of net
in contrasting colors*

3 sugared almonds

*18in (45cm) length of ribbon,
¼in (6mm) wide*

A few sugared almonds wrapped in colored net make a sophisticated-looking tree decoration—with the added bonus that you can give them away to friends and visitors over the festive season.

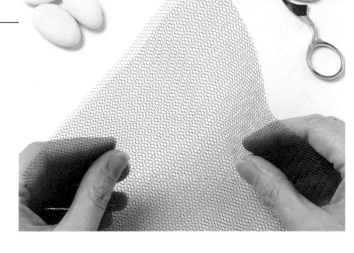

1 | Place the two net squares one on top of the other.

2 | Place the three almonds in the center of the net squares and bring up the corners to form a neat bag.

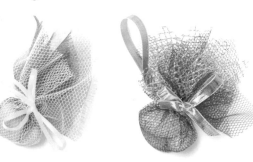

3 | Fold the ribbon in half and make a single stitch about 10cm (4in) from the fold. Hold the ribbon loop behind the almond bunch and tie the loose ends at the front in a bow.

Decorated Cookies

YOU WILL NEED

BASIC RECIPE

For the cookies:

3oz (75g) butter

1½oz (40g) fine granulated sugar

1oz (25g) cornstarch

3oz (75g) all-purpose flour

FOR THE WATER ICING

8oz (250g) confectioner's sugar

6 dessertspoons warm water

EQUIPMENT

Drinking straws

Palette knife

Children will enjoy helping to decorate these Christmas cookies. The cookies should be eaten within a week of being made—though you probably won't be able to resist them for that long!

1 Make the cookies following the instructions on page 238. While still warm, push a short length of a drinking straw into the top of each cookie shape to make a hole for hanging. Leave the straw in place.

2 Using a palette knife, put a small amount of water icing in the middle of each shape. Working quickly before the cookies cool, spread the icing evenly over the top and sides. Mix together the confectioner's sugar and water to the consistency of pouring cream.

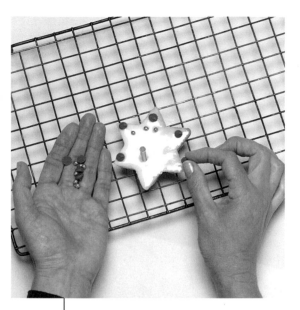

3 Decorate the cookies with chocolate chips and silver cake decorations. Leave to cool. Store in an airtight container for two days to allow the icing to harden.

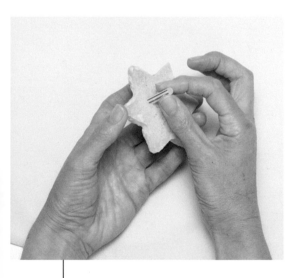

4 Remove the drinking straws by pushing them through the back of the cookies from the front (if you pull out the straws from the front, you may crack the icing).

5 Fold a ribbon length in half and push the folded end through the hole in the cookie from the back. Feed the cut ends through the loop and pull tight. Tie the cut ends together to form a loop for hanging and cut off any excess ribbon on the diagonal to neaten.

Piped Chocolate Treats

YOU WILL NEED

Chocolate

Butter

Heavy cream

Yolk of 1 egg

Petit-fours cases

Wax paper

Adhesive tape

Fluted nozzle

An easy and delicious chocolate filling can be quickly whipped up by melting chocolate over a pan of hot water, and then stirring in a cube of butter, one egg yolk and a little heavy cream. Beat the mixture and leave it to cool before using to fill meringues, decorate petit-fours, to pipe onto cakes, or to make the cups shown here.

1 Making chocolate cups: To make the filling, melt chocolate over a pan of boiling water and then add butter, cream and egg yolk and beat well.

2 Melt more chocolate and, using a spoon, coat the insides of small petit-fours cases. Allow to set, then apply a second coat.

3 Place the cases in a cool place to allow the second coat of chocolate to set, then peel away the cases to reveal the chocolate 'cups'.

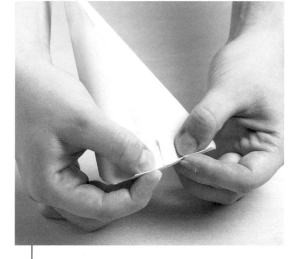

6 Turn in the corners at the open end of the cone and crease to secure. A paper clip or adhesive tape will keep them in place.

4 Making a piping bag: Make a 10 x 4in (25 x 10cm) rectangle from waxproof paper. Fold the paper diagonally in half to form two triangular shapes.

5 Fold the blunt end of the triangle to create a pointed cone. Bring over the other end, making the pointed as possible.

7 Fit a fluted nozzle then fill the piping bag with chocolate filling, and pipe it into the cases. Decorate as desired.

Templates *and* Recipes

Templates

COPPER CANDLE SCONCE, PAGE 15.

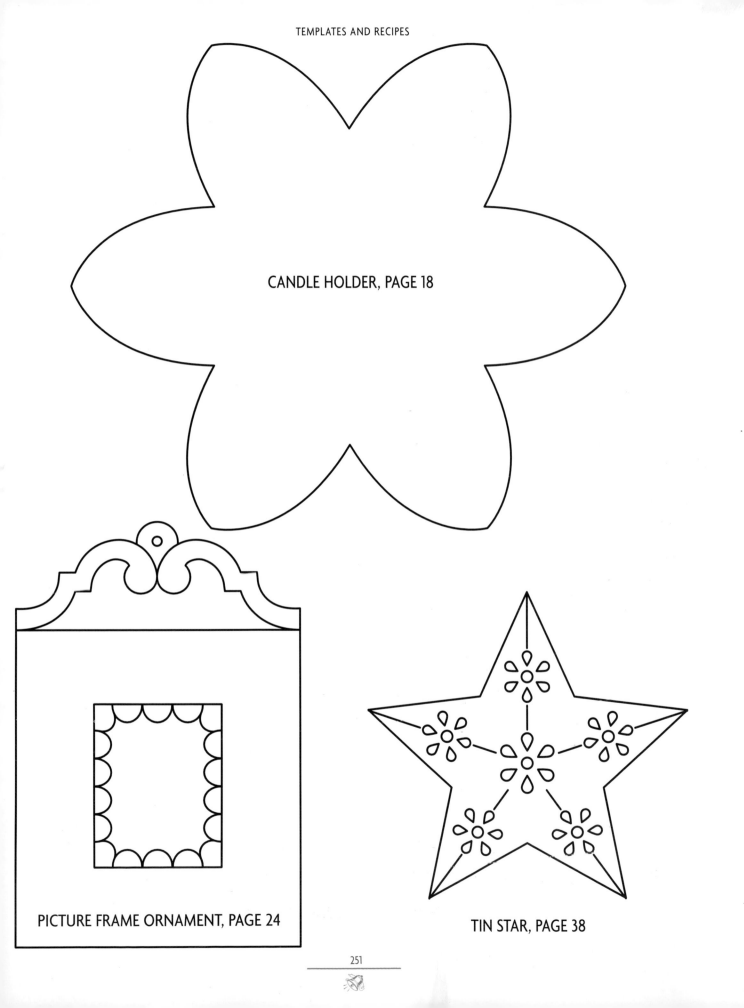

CANDLE HOLDER, PAGE 18

PICTURE FRAME ORNAMENT, PAGE 24

TIN STAR, PAGE 38

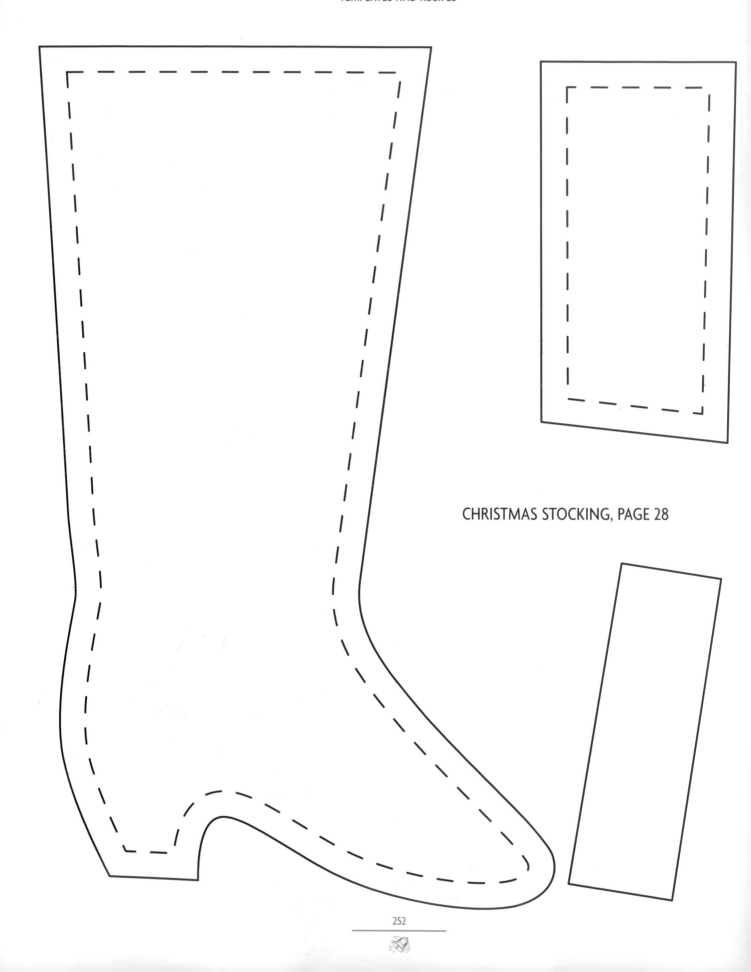

CHRISTMAS STOCKING, PAGE 28

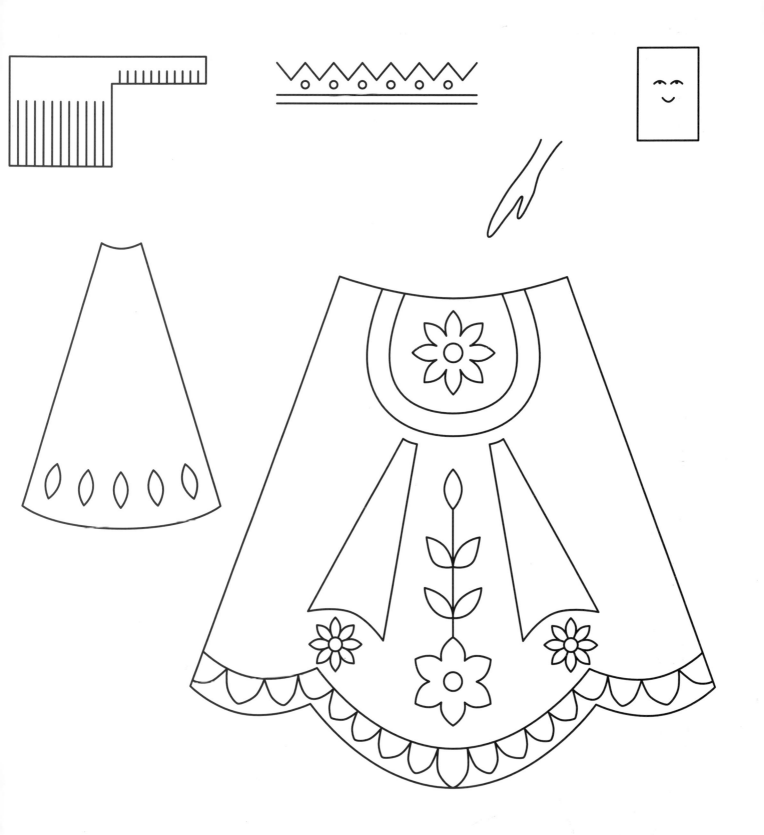

TIN ANGEL, PAGE 40

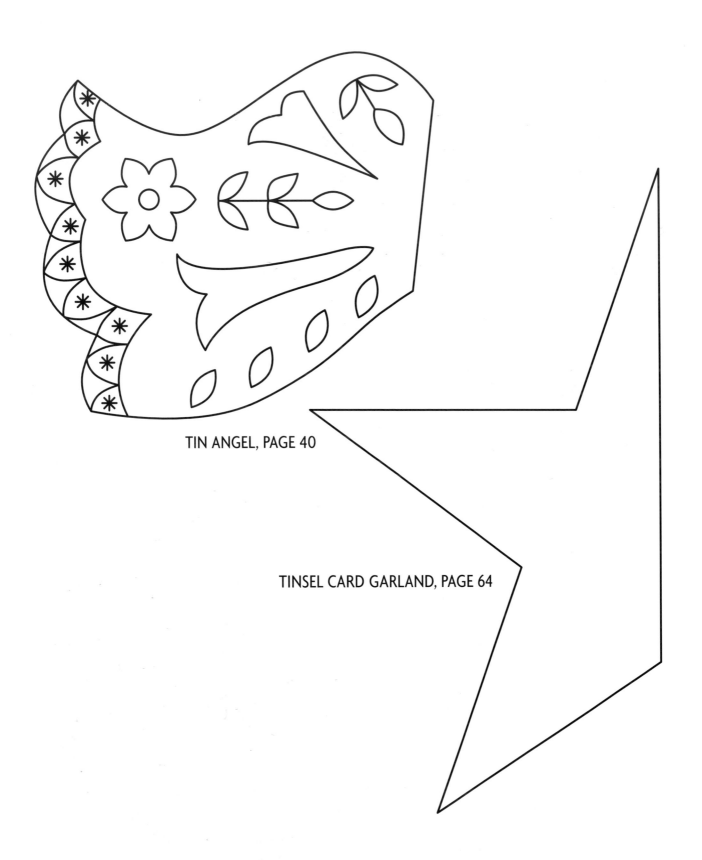

TIN ANGEL, PAGE 40

TINSEL CARD GARLAND, PAGE 64

BEADED RAINBOW CATCHER DESIGNS,
PAGE 70. ENLARGE TO 200%

FELT CHRISTMAS TREE, PAGE 66

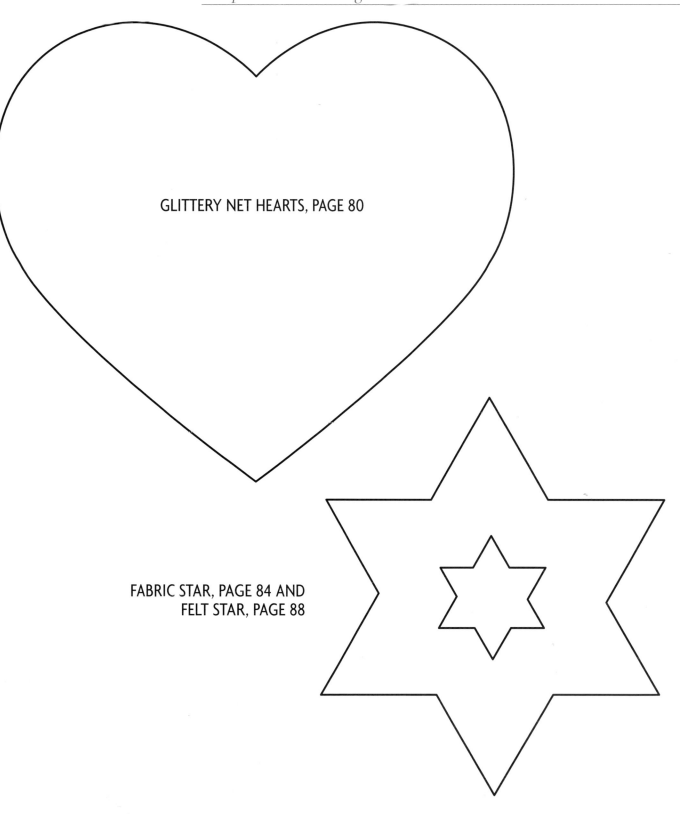

GLITTERY NET HEARTS, PAGE 80

FABRIC STAR, PAGE 84 AND
FELT STAR, PAGE 88

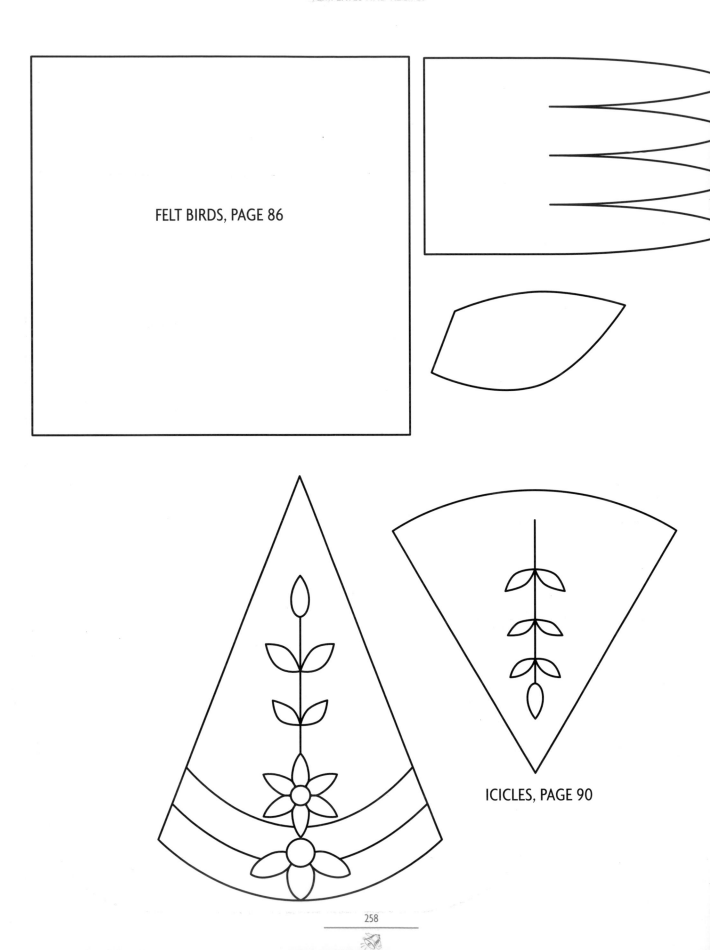

FELT BIRDS, PAGE 86

ICICLES, PAGE 90

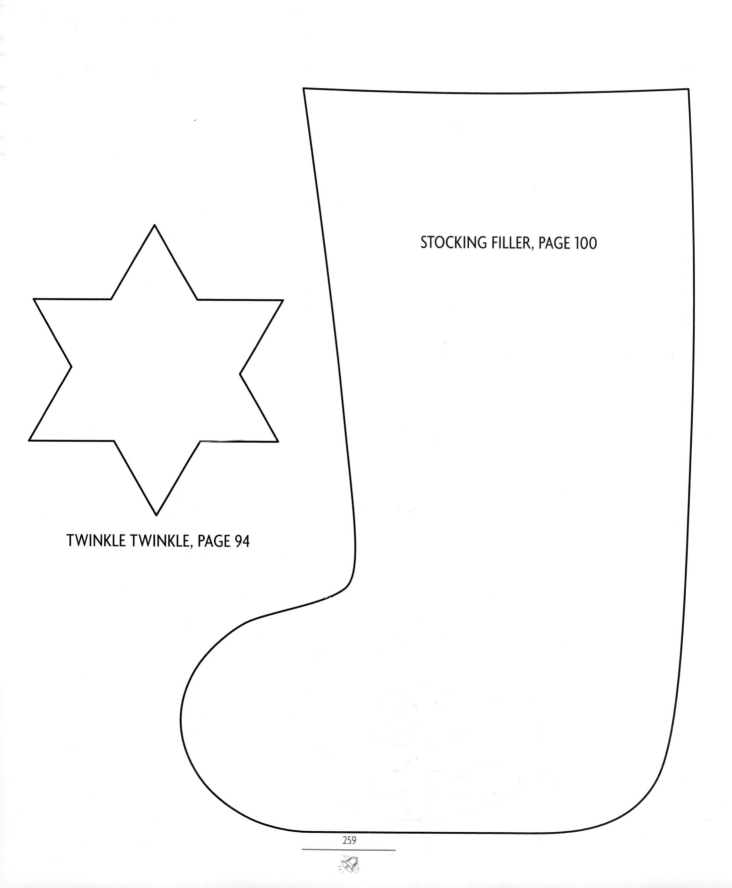

STOCKING FILLER, PAGE 100

TWINKLE TWINKLE, PAGE 94

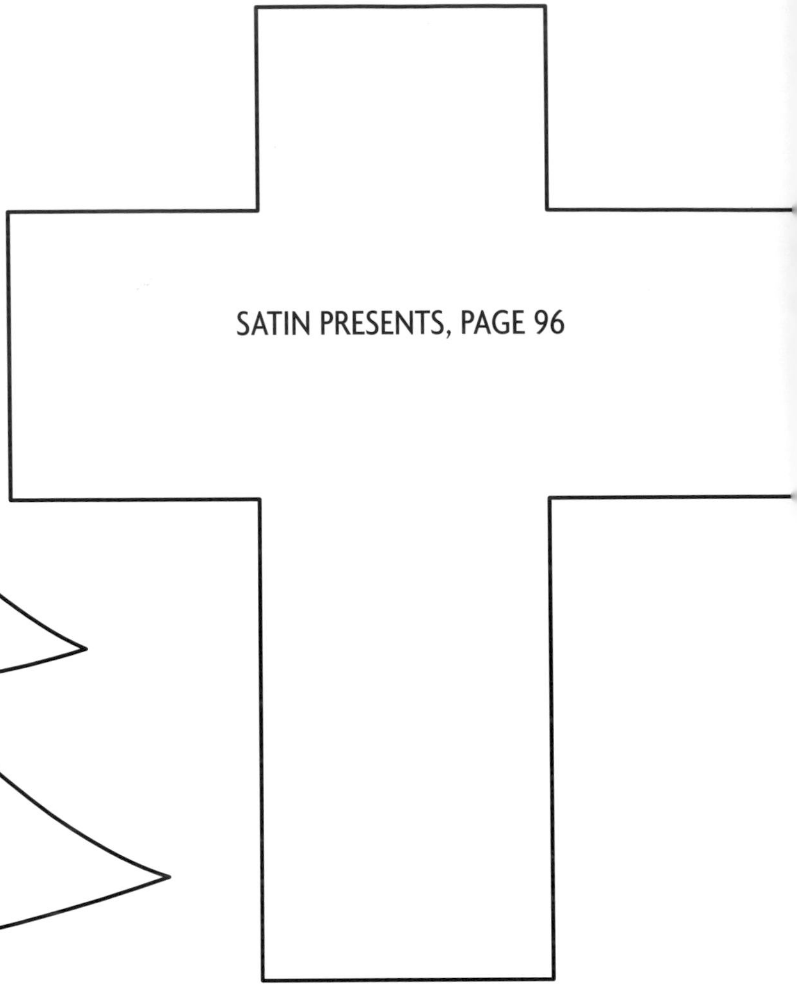

SATIN PRESENTS, PAGE 96

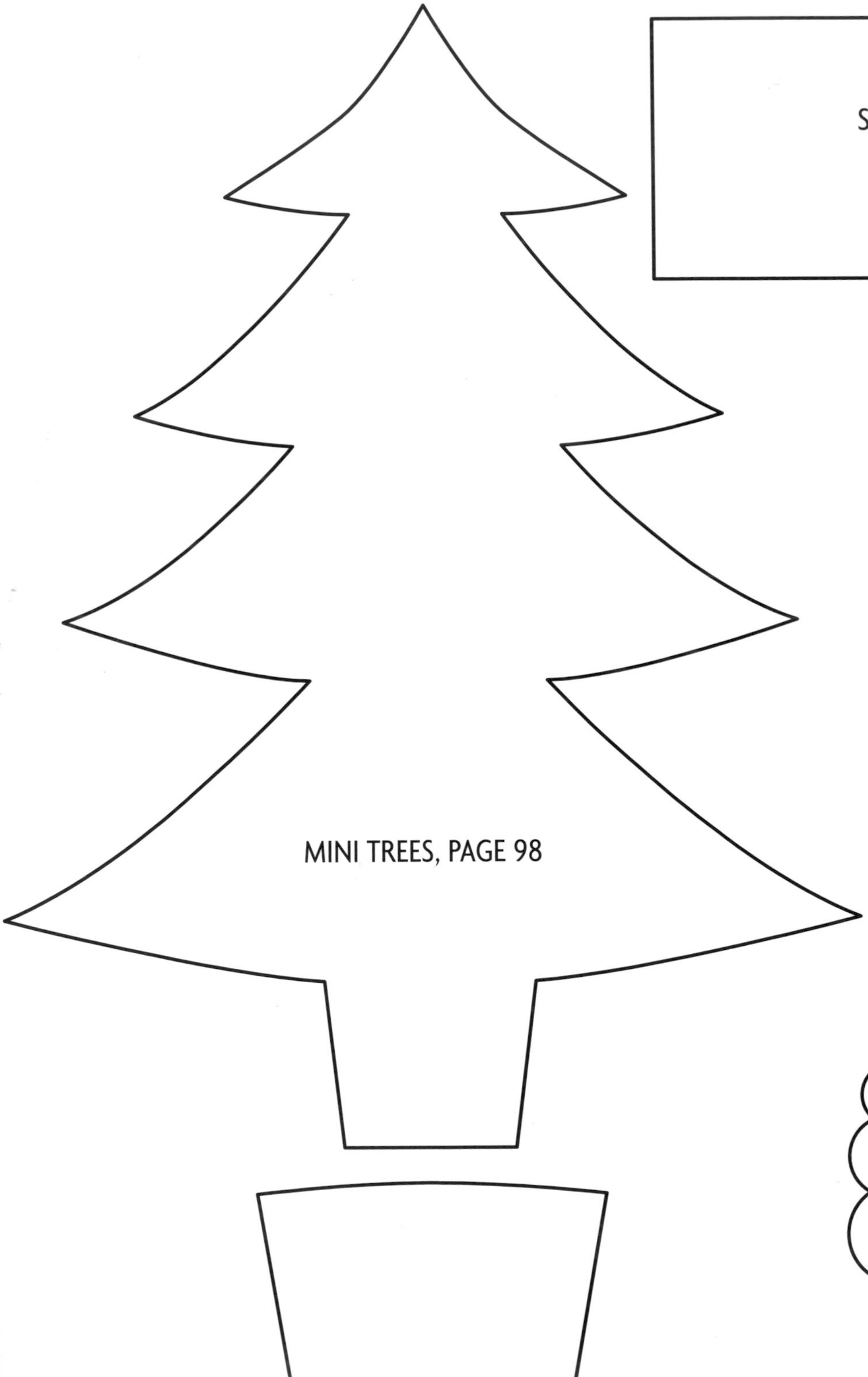

MINI TREES, PAGE 98

SANTA FACES, PAGE 97

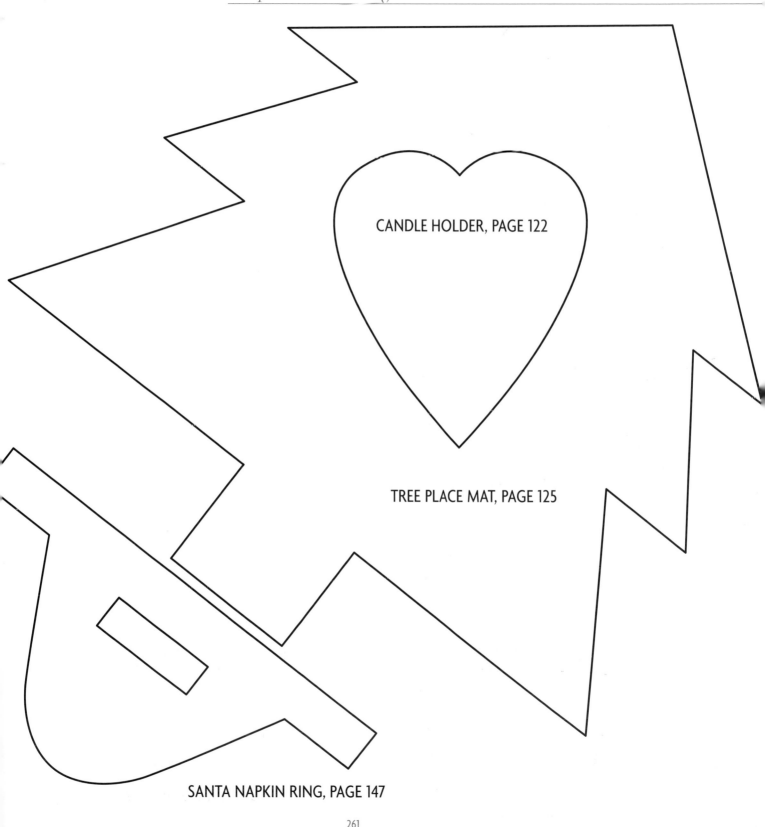

CANDLE HOLDER, PAGE 122

TREE PLACE MAT, PAGE 125

SANTA NAPKIN RING, PAGE 147

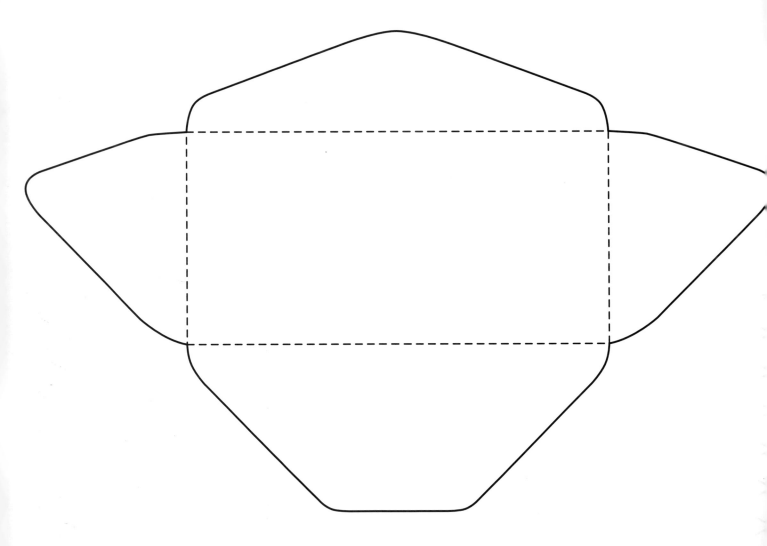

MAKING ENVELOPES, PAGE 160

CHRISTMAS GIFT BOX, PAGE 154

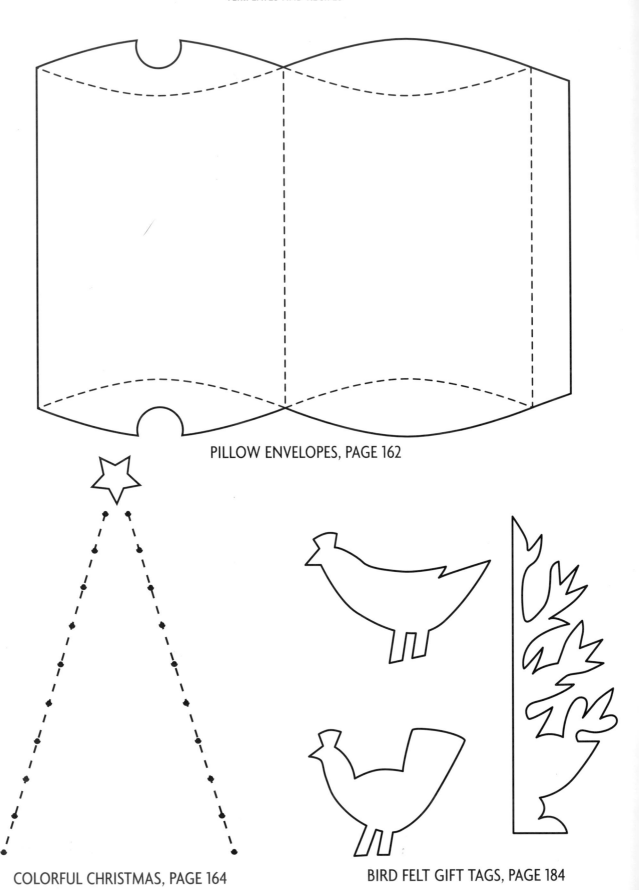

PILLOW ENVELOPES, PAGE 162

COLORFUL CHRISTMAS, PAGE 164

BIRD FELT GIFT TAGS, PAGE 184

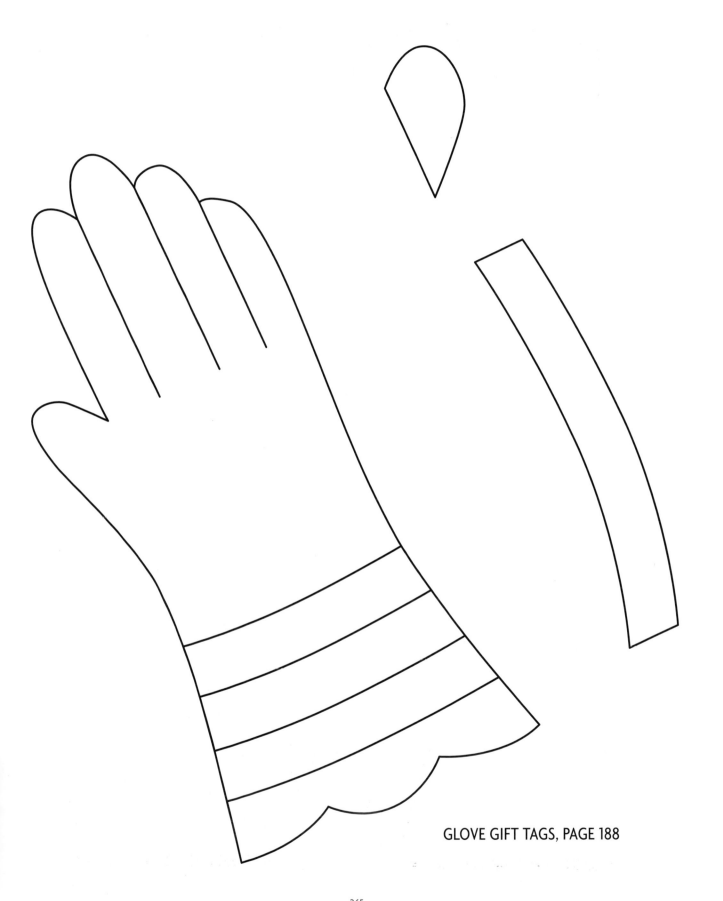

GLOVE GIFT TAGS, PAGE 188

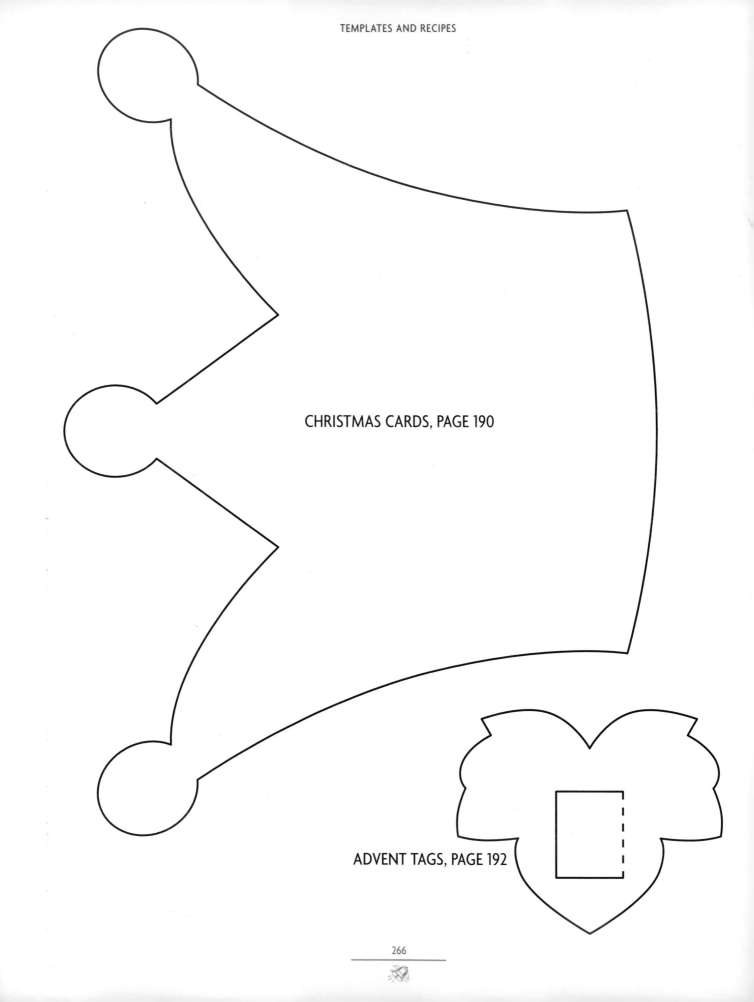

CHRISTMAS CARDS, PAGE 190

ADVENT TAGS, PAGE 192

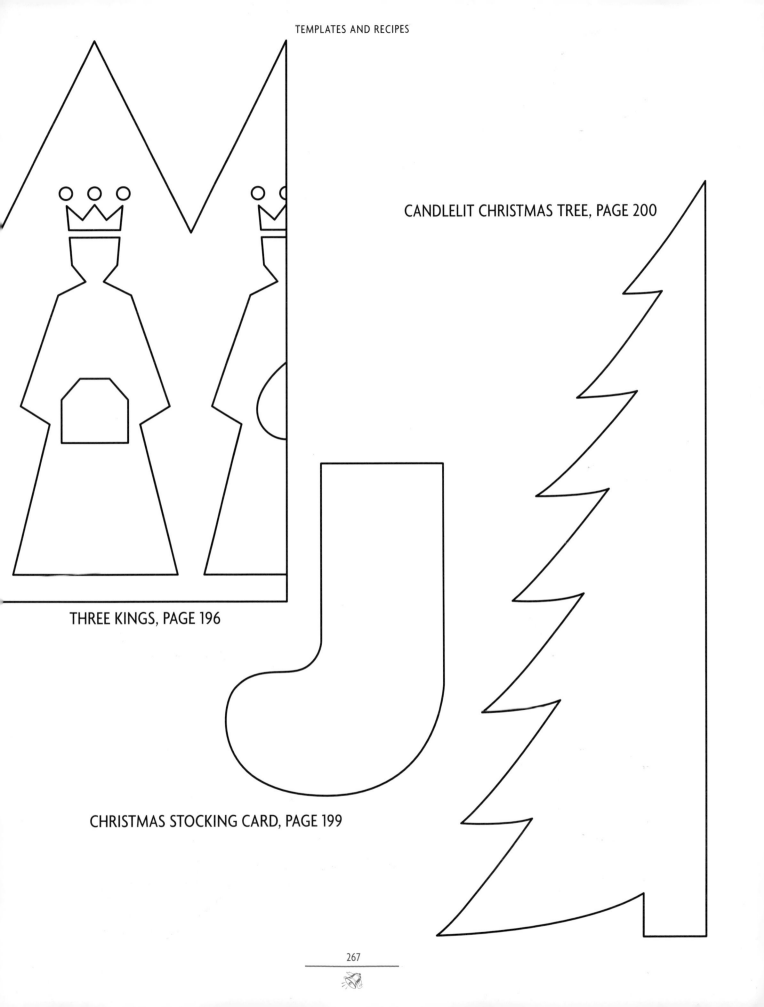

CANDLELIT CHRISTMAS TREE, PAGE 200

THREE KINGS, PAGE 196

CHRISTMAS STOCKING CARD, PAGE 199

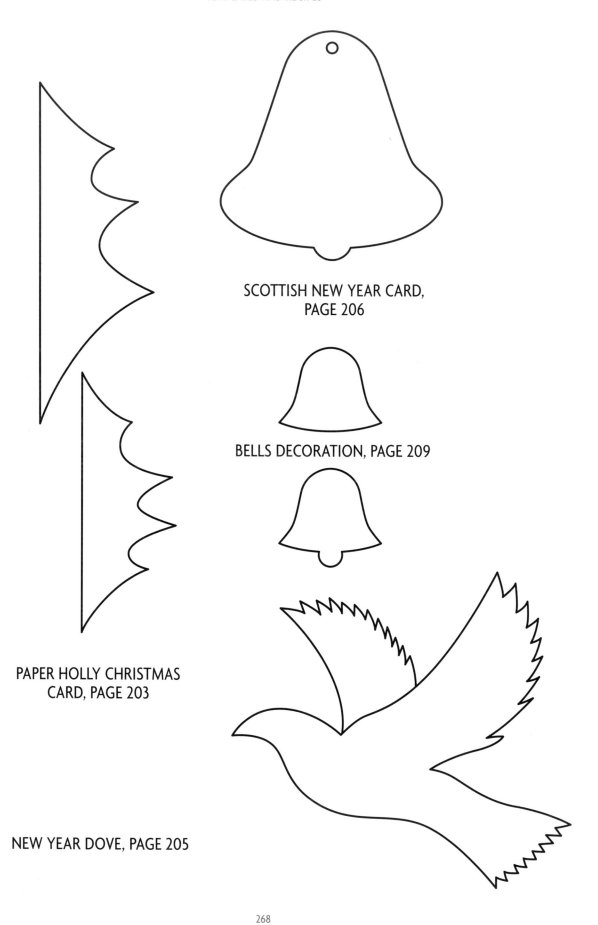

SCOTTISH NEW YEAR CARD,
PAGE 206

BELLS DECORATION, PAGE 209

PAPER HOLLY CHRISTMAS
CARD, PAGE 203

NEW YEAR DOVE, PAGE 205

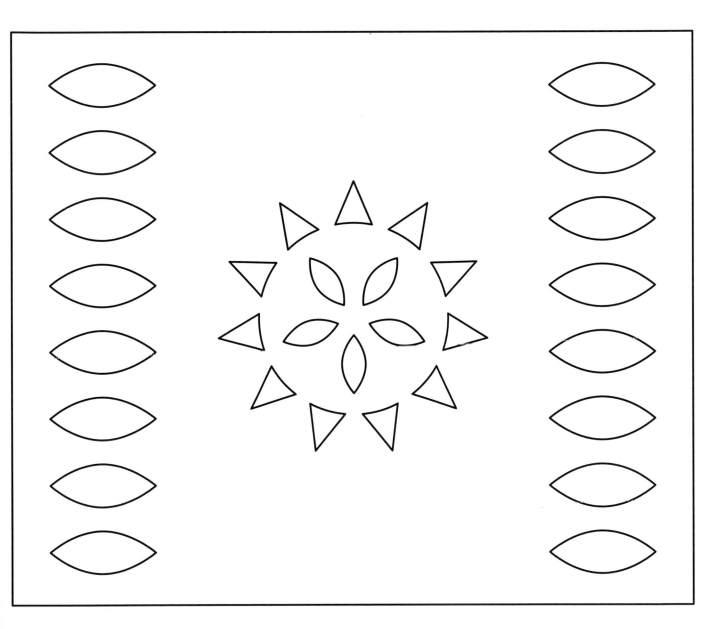

AMARETTO WRAPPERS, PAGE 222

SNOWFLAKE SEWING BOX, PAGE 224

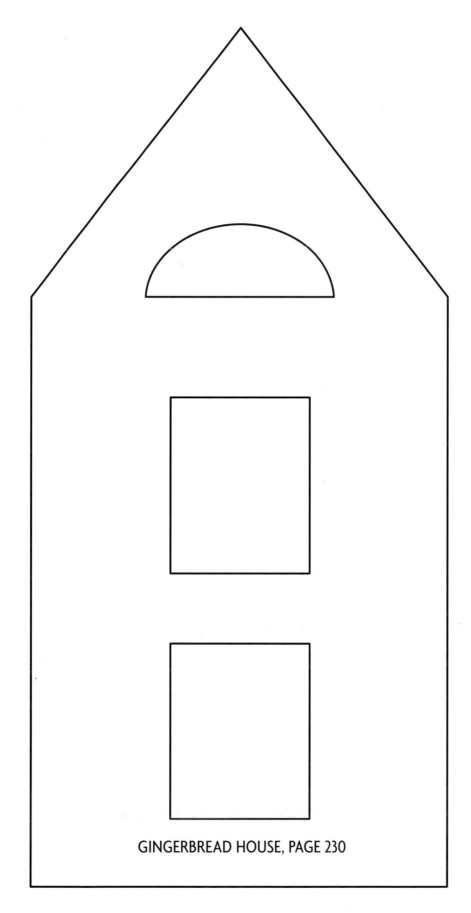

GINGERBREAD HOUSE, PAGE 230

GINGERBREAD HOUSE, PAGE 230

GINGERBREAD HOUSE, PAGE 230

Recipes

SALT DOUGH

Ingredients

4 cups flour

1 cup salt

1-½ cups hot water

2 teaspoons vegetable oil (optional)

Method

Mix the salt and flour together, then gradually add the water until the dough becomes elastic. (Some recipes call for 2 teaspoons of vegetable oil at this point.) If your mixture turns out too sticky, simply add more flour. If it turns out too crumbly, simply add more water.

Knead the dough until it's a good consistency—then get out rolling pins, cups, bowls, straws, cookie cutters, plastic utensils, and let the fun begin!

If you want colored dough, mix food coloring, powdered drink mix, or paint into the water before adding it to the dry ingredients. Or you can paint your creations after baking them at 400°F/200°C/gas 6. Baking times will vary depending on the size and thickness of the object, but make sure that all of it is hard. If the dough starts to darken before cooking is complete, cover with aluminum foil. Painted keepsakes will need to be sealed on all sides with clear varnish or polyurethane spray.

PASTRY

Ingredients

4oz fat (125g)

8oz flour (250g)

Pinch of salt

Water

Note: If you are making sweet pastry, for a fruit pie for example, add 2oz (50g) of caster sugar to 3oz of fat (75g) and use an egg rather than water.

Method

Sift the flour and salt (allowing ½-1 level teaspoons. salt per 8oz of flour.) Cut the fat into small pieces and rub into the flour using the tips of your fingers.

Rub until the mixture looks like fine breadcrumbs. Using a knife, mix to a stiff dough with about 2-3 tablespoons of water. Too much water and too soft a pastry will make it tough and hard when baked. Try not to knead the pastry as this can also make it tough.

Sprinkle flour on a board and rolling pin, and roll out with light quick rolls. When scraps of pastry need to be re-rolled (for instance, when making the base for jam tarts, mince pies etc.) pile the scraps on top of each other and roll lightly.

If possible, leave the pastry in a cool place for 15-30 mins before baking as this will help to reduce any toughness.

AMARETTO COOKIES

Ingredients

4oz (100g) butter

2 tablespoons molasses

2 eggs

1oz (25g) ground toasted almonds

½ teaspoon grated lemon rind

1 teaspoon almond extract

4oz (100g) amaretto

1lb 1½oz (500g) wholewheat pastry flour

Method

Cream together the butter and molasses. Add the eggs, ground almonds, lemon rind and almond extract, mix well. Stir in the amaretto alternately with flour. Drop by teaspoonsful onto unoiled cookie sheets. Bake at 350°F/180°C/gas 4 for 12-15 minutes. The cookies will be golden brown when done. This recipe makes 36 cookies.

Bake in a hot oven around 400°F/200°C/gas 6 for 20 minutes or until it reaches the preferred shade of golden brown. Obviously if cooking a pie or tart the cooking time may vary depending on the filling.

TRADITIONAL CHRISTMAS CAKE

Ingredients

1lb (450g) currants

6oz (175g) sultanas

6oz (175g) raisins

2oz (50g) glace cherries, rinsed, dried and finely chopped

2oz (50g) mixed candied peel, finely chopped

3 tablespoons brandy

8oz (225g) plain flour

teaspoon salt

teaspoon freshly grated nutmeg

teaspoon ground mixed spice

8oz (225g) unsalted butter

8oz (225g) soft brown sugar

2oz (50g) almonds, chopped (the skins can be left on)

1 dessertspoon black treacle

The grated zest of 1 lemon

The grated zest of 1 orange

4oz (110g) whole blanched almonds (only if you don't intend to ice the cake)

4 Eggs

You will need an 8in (20cm) round cake tin or a 7in (18cm) square tin, eased and lined with greaseproof paper. Tie a band of brown paper round the outside of the tin for extra protection.

Method

This recipe works best if you begin this cake the night before you want to bake it.

Weigh out the dried fruit and mixed peel, place it in a mixing bowl and mix in the brandy as evenly and thoroughly as possible. Cover the bowl with a clean tea-cloth and leave the fruit aside to absorb the brandy for 12 hours.

Next day pre-heat the oven to 275°F/140°C/gas 2. Then measure out all the rest of the ingredients (the treacle will be easier to measure if you remove the lid and place the tin in a small pan of barely simmering water).

Begin the cake by sifting the flour, salt and spices into a large mixing bowl.

Next, in a separate large mixing bowl, whisk the butter and sugar together until it's light, pale and fluffy.

Now beat the eggs in a separate bowl and add them to the creamed mixture a tablespoonful at a time; keep the whisk running until all the egg is incorporated.

When all the egg has been added fold in the flour and spices, using gentle, folding movements and not beating at all (this is to keep the air in). Now fold in the fruit, peel, chopped nuts and treacle and finally the grated lemon and orange zests.

Using a large wooden spoon, put the cake mixture into the prepared tin, spread it out evenly with the back of the spoon and, if you don't intend to ice the cake, lightly drop the whole blanched almonds on the top.

Finally cover the top of the cake with a square of greaseproof paper with a coin sized hole in the centre (this gives extra protection during the long cooking).

Bake the cake on the lowest shelf of the oven for 4 to 4½ hours. Sometimes it can take up to half an hour longer than this, but in any case don't look till at least 4 hours have passed.

Cool the cake for 30 minutes in the tin, then remove it to a wire rack to finish cooling. When it's cold pour on some Brandy or Sherry, then wrap it in double greaseproof paper secured with an elastic band and either wrap again in foil or store in an airtight tin. You can now add further Brandy or Sherry at intervals until you need to ice or eat it.

ALMOND PASTE

Almond paste is used between the icing and a rich fruit cake to prevent the icing discoloring.

Ingredients

This recipe makes about 450g (1lb).
4oz (100g) icing sugar
4oz (100g) caster sugar
8oz (225g) ground almonds
1 teaspoon vanilla flavoring
1-2 tablespoon lemon juice
1 egg, beaten

Method

Sift the icing sugar into a bowl and stir in the caster sugar and ground almonds.

Add the flavoring and 15 ml (1 tablespoon) lemon juice, then work in the egg with more lemon juice if needed to form a stiff paste. Form into a ball and knead lightly.

Applying the Almond Paste

Measure round the cake with a piece of string. Dust the working surface with icing sugar.

Roll out two-thirds of the paste to a rectangle, half the length of the string by twice the depth of the cake. Trim the rectangle and cut in half lengthways.

Place the cake upside down on a board and brush the sides with apricot glaze.

Gently lift the almond paste and place it firmly in position round the cake. Smooth the joins with a palette knife and keep the top and bottom edges square. Roll a jam jar lightly round the cake to help the paste stick.

Brush the top of the cake with apricot glaze and roll out the remaining almond paste to fit. With the help of the rolling pin, lift it carefully on to the cake. Lightly roll with the rolling pin, then smooth the join and leave to dry for 2-5 days before starting to ice.

ROYAL ICING

Ingredients

2 egg whites

1lb (450g) icing sugar

1 teaspoon lemon juice

1 teaspoon glycerine

This recipe makes about 1lb (450g).

Method

Whisk the egg whites in a bowl until slightly frothy. Sift and stir in about a quarter of the icing sugar with a wooden spoon. Continue adding more sugar gradually, beating well after each addition, until about three-quarters of the sugar has been added altogether.

Beat in the lemon juice and continue beating for about 10 minutes until the icing is smooth.

Beat in the remaining sugar until the required consistency is achieved, depending on how the icing will be used.

Finally, stir in the glycerine to prevent the icing hardening.

Cover and keep for 24 hours to allow air bubbles to rise to the surface.

MOULDING ICING

Ingredients

1lb (450g) icing sugar

1 egg white

2oz (50g) liquid glucose

coloring

flavoring (vanilla or lemon)

This recipe makes about 1lb (450g).

Method

Sift the icing sugar into a mixing bowl and make a well in the centre.

Add the egg white and glucose. Beat, gradually drawing the icing sugar into the centre of the bowl, until the mixture is quite stiff.

Knead the icing, incorporating any remaining icing sugar, until smooth and manageable.

Add coloring and flavoring and a little more icing sugar if necessary.

Store the icing in a sealed polythene bag or container in a cool place to prevent it drying.

How To Use Moulded Icing to Cover a Cake

Roll out the icing to a round or square 5 cm (2 inches) larger than the cake.

Lift the icing on the rolling pin and place on top of the marzipan-covered cake.

Press the icing on to the side of the cake, working the

surplus to the base.

Lightly dust your hands in icing sugar and rub the top and sides in a circular movement to make it smooth.

Cut off the surplus icing at the base.

How to Ice a Cake

Always apply royal icing over a layer of almond paste rather than directly on to the cake.

Stand the cake and board on a non-slip surface. Spoon almost half the icing on to the top of the cake and spread it evenly over the surface with a palette knife, using a paddling action.

Using an icing ruler or palette knife longer than the width of the cake, without applying any pressure, draw it steadily across the top of the cake at an angle of 30°. Repeat if necessary.

Neaten the edges by holding a palette knife upright and running it around the rim of the cake to remove surplus icing. Leave to dry for about 24 hours before applying icing to side of cake. Cover remaining icing.

Place cake on an icing turntable or upturned plate.

Spread remaining icing on the side and smooth roughly with a small palette knife, using a paddling action as for the top of the cake.

Hold the palette knife upright and at an angle of 45° to the cake. Draw the knife or comb towards you to smooth the surface. For a square cake, apply icing to each side separately.

Neaten the edges with a palette knife. Reserve the surplus icing for decorating.

For a really smooth finish, allow to dry for 1 to 2 days, then thin icing with a little water, and apply this as a second coat. Use a sharp knife to trim off any rough icing. Use sandpaper to sand down any imperfections in the first coat.

Brush surface with grease free pastry brush to remove icing dust. Leave to dry thoroughly before adding piped decorations.

Suppliers

US

Kate's Paperie
Retailers of all types of paper and card blanks for use in general papercrafts and craftmaking.
561 Broadway
New York
NY 10012
Tel: 800 809 9880
Website: http://www.katespaperie.com

Swallow Creek Papers
Retailers of fine papers in a variety of treatments and prints.
PO Box 152
Spring Mills
PA 16875
Tel: 814 422 8651

Flax Art & Design
Large supply of papers and cardmaking equipment.
1699 Market Street
San Francisco
CA 94103
Tel: 415 552 2355
Email: info@flaxart.com
Website: http://www.flaxart.com

Michaels
Art and craft materials of all kinds.
Tel: 800 642 4235
Website: http://www.michaels.com

Pearl Paint Co Inc
Retailers of art and craft materials.
308 Canal Street
New York
NY 10013
Tel: 800 451 7327
Website: http://www.pearlpaint.com

Sunshine Discount Crafts
Online catalogue of discount craft supplies and products.
12335 62nd St
N Largo
FL 33773
Tel: 800 729 2878
Email: customercare@sunshinecrafts.com
Website: http://www.sunshinecrafts.com

Create For Less
Stock over 50,000 brand name craft supplies.
6932 SW Macadam Avenue
Suite A

Portland
OR 97219
Tel: 866 333 4463
Email: info@createforless.com
Website: http://www.createforless.com

Craft Catalog

Huge selection of supplies, including wood
& wore, acrylic paints, brushes, and paper
mâché equipment.
PO Box 1069
Reynoldsburg
OH 43068
Tel: 800 777 1442
Email: sales@craftcatalog.com
Website: http://www.craftcatalog.com

The Stampin' Place

Huge selection of rubber art stamps and
accessories for general arts and crafts.
PO Box 43
Big Lake
MN 44309
Tel: 800 634 3717
Email: feedback@stampin.com
Website: http://www.stampin.com

Creative Crafts and Hobbies

Art supplies at wholesale prices for huge
selection of crafting activities.
808-814 Westport Road
Kansas City
Missouri
64111
Tel: 816 531 1213
Website: www.creativecraftsandhobbies.com

Ecstasy Crafts

Supply products for papercraft projects,
including cardmaking, paper tole, and
paper weaving.
PO Box 525
Watertown
NY 13601
Tel: 888 288 7131
Email: info@ecstasycrafts.com
Website: http://www.ecstasycrafts.com

A.C. Moore

A vast assortment of arts, crafts, and florals
at competitive prices.
Website: http://www.acmoore.com

CANADA

Lewiscraft
Canadian craft experts.
Across Canada.
Website: http://www.lewiscraft.ca

MacPherson Art & Craft Supplies
91 Queen Street East
St Marys
Ontario
N4X 1C2
Tel: 519 284 1741
Fax: 519 284 0858
Toll-free: 800 238 6663
Email: info@macphersoncrafts.com
Website:
http://www.macphersoncrafts.com

Alberta Bees Wax & Candlemaking Supplies
10611 170th St
Edmonton
Alberta
T5P 4WZ
Tel: 780 413 0350
Fax: 780 481 3228
Email: sales@candlesandbeeswax.com
Website:
http://www.candlesandbeeswax.com

Cake Walk Decorating & Supplies
12918 117th St
Edmonton
Alberta
T5E 5J7
Tel: 780 455 2608
Email: chris@cake-walk.ca
Website: http://www.cake-walk.ca

Aboveground Art Supplies
74 McCaul Street
Toronto
Ontario
M5T 3K2
Tel: 416 591 1601
Fax: 416 591 2171
Toll-free: 800 591 1615
Website:
http://www.aboveGroundartsupplies.com

Omnicrafts
2215 Plesser Street
Ottawa
Ontario
K1G 2X2
Tel: 613 795 4197
Email: info@omnicrafts.com
Website: http://www.omnicrafts.com

All That Stuff Party Supplies
2479 Jeans Way
Nanaimo
British Columbia
V9T 3W9
Tel: 250 758 7184
Fax: 250 758 7168
Toll-free: 888 332 4224
Email: sales@allthatstuff.net
Website: http://www.allthatstuff.net

Canadian Craft Supplies
32 Major Street
Dartmouth
Nova Scotia
B2X 1A6
Tel: 902 000 0000
Fax 902 435 9184
Email: sales@canadiancraftsupplies.com
Website:
http://www.canadiancraftsupplies.com

Michaels
Art and craft materials of all kinds.
Tel: 800 642 4235
Website: http://www.michaels.com

Index

Acknowledgments

Alan and Barry would like to thank all the

contributors whose projects have been featured in

this book, notably Claire Leavey, Carol

McCleeve, Stephanie Donaldson, Simon Lycett,

Deborah Schneebeli-Morrell, and Sarah

Beaman. They would also like to thank Miranda

Sessions, Marie Clayton, and Katie Cowan at

Collins & Brown for their enthusiasm and

support in putting this book together.

Thanks one and all.